Words Th  ay

Words Sorts for Derivational Relations Spellers

Francine Johnston
University of North Carolina at Greensboro

Donald R. Bear
University of Nevada, Reno

Marcia Invernizzi
University of Virginia

PEARSON

Merrill
Prentice Hall

Upper Saddle River, New Jersey
Columbus, Ohio

Vice President and Executive Publisher: Jeffery W. Johnston
Senior Editor: Linda Ashe Montgomery
Editorial Assistant: Laura Weaver
Development Editor: Hope Madden
Production Editor: Mary M. Irvin
Design Coordinator: Diane C. Lorenzo
Cover Designer: Ali Mohrman
Cover Image: Jean Claude Lejuene
Production Manager: Pamela D. Bennett
Director of Marketing: Ann Castel Davis
Marketing Manager: Darcy Betts Prybella
Marketing Coordinator: Tyra Poole

This book was set in Palatino by Carlisle Communications, Ltd. It was printed and bound by Courier Kendallville, Inc. The cover was printed by Coral Graphics.

Pearson Prentice Hall™ is a trademark of Pearson Education, Inc.
Pearson® is a registered trademark of Pearson plc
Prentice Hall® is a registered trademark of Pearson Education, Inc.
Merrill® is a registered trademark of Pearson Education, Inc.

Pearson Education Ltd.
Pearson Education Singapore Pte. Ltd.
Pearson Education Canada, Ltd.
Pearson Education—Japan

Pearson Education Australia Pty. Limited
Pearson Education North Asia Ltd.
Pearson Educación de Mexico, S.A. de C.V.
Pearson Education Malaysia Pte. Ltd.

10 9 8 7 6 5 4 3 2

0-13-171812-6

Contents

Overview   1

SORTS 1-4
Prefixes and Suffixes   7

SORTS 5-8
Spelling-Meaning Patterns I   17

SORTS 9-19
Spelling-Meaning Patterns II   27

SORTS 20-28
Greek and Latin Elements I   49

SORTS 29-34
Greek and Latin Elements II   69

SORTS 35-43
Greek and Latin Elements III   83

SORTS 44-50
Advanced Spelling-Meaning Patterns   101

Appendix   115

Preface

Words Their Way: Word Sorts for Derivational Relations Spellers is intended to complement the text *Words Their Way: Word Study for Phonics, Vocabulary, and Spelling Instruction*. That core text provides a practical, research-based, and classroom-proven way to study words with students. This companion text expands and enriches that word study, specifically for derivational relations spellers.

Word study for advanced readers and writers focuses on the way spelling and vocabulary knowledge at this stage grow primarily through processes of derivation—from a single base word or word root, a number of related words are derived through the addition of prefixes and suffixes. Advanced readers, for example, are able to explore Latin and Greek word elements that are the important morphemes out of which thousands of words are constructed. This leads naturally to an exploration of spelling-meaning relationships.

Words Their Way: Word Sorts for Derivational Relations Spellers provides teachers with prepared reproducible sorts and step-by-step directions to guide students through the sorting lessons. There are organizational tips as well as follow-up activities to extend the lesson through weekly routines. The materials provided in this text will complement the use of any existing spelling and reading curricula.

More resources for word study in the derivational relations stage, including resources for using word study with students who speak Spanish, links to websites related to word study, as well as information about the *Words Their Way* CD-ROM, Video, other companion materials, and word study events can be found on the text's Companion Website. You can link to this site at

www.prenhall.com/bear

Overview

PLACEMENT

This collection of word sorts is for students who are in the derivational relations stage of spelling development. These students should already have a firm understanding of common syllable juncture patterns, spelling patterns within stressed and unstressed syllables in two-syllable words, and the effects of common prefixes and suffixes on the base words to which they are affixed. These students are often in the upper elementary grades, but fall primarily at the middle school level and up. To determine exactly where individual students should start, administer one of the spelling inventories described in Chapter 2 of *Words Their Way*. The *Intermediate Spelling Inventory* and the *Upper Level Spelling Inventory* will help you determine more precisely where students at these levels should begin with their word study. Both of these inventories may be found in the appendix of *Words Their Way*, 3rd Edition; the *Intermediate Spelling Inventory* is on pages 308–310 and the *Upper Level Spelling Inventory* is on pages 311–316.

OVERVIEW OF CONTENT

Word study at the derivational relations stage focuses primarily on the *structure* or *morphology* of written words. Students systematically examine how the spelling of words visually represents meaning units, or *morphemes*. Students at this level are fairly competent spellers, so the errors they make are "higher level," requiring a more advanced foundation of spelling and vocabulary knowledge to address. Because of this more advanced level of word knowledge, word study at the derivational relations stage focuses as much on *vocabulary* development as it does on *spelling* development. Analyzing the spelling of words supports vocabulary growth, and vocabulary growth in trun provides helpful support for higher-level spelling development.

Vocabulary grows and develops in many ways. It is well established that certain words need to be taught systematically and deeply; that students need to do a lot of reading in order to experience and acquire over time the broad sweep of English vocabulary; and that students need to learn the processes whereby meaningful word elements or morphemes—prefixes, suffixes, base words, and word roots—combine. Linguists refer to the last type of knowledge as *generative*: Once students understand the basics according to which these important word parts combine, they can apply this knowledge to determining or *generating* the spelling and meaning of literally thousands of words. Linguists estimate that 60%–80% of English vocabulary is created through these processes of word combination; therefore, students who understand these processes will be well equipped to analyze and learn most of the unfamiliar words they will encounter in their reading and their study in specific content areas.

Because this supplement focuses on *generative* word knowledge in spelling and vocabulary, most of the word sorts include both familiar and unfamiliar words. Knowledge of the meaning of the known words or of the meaningful word parts in the known words will enable students in most instances to infer the meanings of the unfamiliar words.

This supplement includes 50 sorts partitioned into six sections. In general, the sorts are sequenced according to morphological complexity. Early on, students examine spelling/meaning patterns as these occur primarily in known words before moving to the examination of Greek and Latin affixes and roots in later sorts. In the first set of sorts students will review basic processes of affixation—adding prefixes and suffixes—in words that are appropriate for examination at this level. Next, spelling-meaning patterns that reflect the process of adding *derivational* suffixes are examined. Spelling-meaning patterns reflect the principle that *words that are related in meaning are often related in spelling as well*. Subsequent sorts interweave spelling-meaning patterns as they occur in words with Greek and Latin word roots and affixes.

Most sorts in this collection present 22–24 words each week. The words have been selected and organized based on patterns of orthographic and morphological, or spelling-meaning, relationships. In each sort, most of the words have been chosen based upon their frequency in reading materials for the intermediate grades and above as well as the spelling and morphological features they represent. Expect students to spell the words in the sort and understand the spelling principles that the sorts reveal. Keep in mind that students at this level are usually what we refer to as "good" spellers, so their developing spelling knowledge supports their vocabulary development. In addition to—or often in place of—assessing spelling, you may wish to assess students' knowledge of the meaning of the words and word parts that have been explored in the sorts. If students are properly placed in the word study curriculum they should already know the meaning of many of the words, be able to spell many of them, and not have to learn 22–24 completely new words in each lesson.

Each section begins with *Notes for the Teacher* and suggestions you can use to introduce and practice the sorts. Importantly, the *Notes for the Teacher* often provide background information about word histories or *etymology* that should be of interest to you and your students. Sorts are presented as blackline masters that can be reproduced for every student to cut apart and use for sorting.

Sorting is an essential instructional routine because it enables students to manipulate words as they look for patterns and relationships. Students should sort their own words several times. We have often heard middle school and high school teachers express doubts about cutting out and sorting words. After they try it, however, they usually find that even older students enjoy the physical sorting process. It is certainly possible to write the sorts instead; but writing is time consuming, and it is not easy to move words to new categories as discoveries are made.

Beginning with sorts 9–19, students sort the words according to their common meaning patterns, which are usually *Latin roots* and *Greek combining forms* shared by the words. The students will then discuss the meanings of the words they know and try to infer the meanings of the roots and combining forms. This inference process is a powerful approach to effective long-term vocabulary building and is also engaging and motivating.

Use the blackline masters to prepare a set of words for modeling. You may want to make a transparency of the sort and cut it apart for use on an overhead, or enlarge the words for use in a pocket chart. You can also simply make your own copy to cut apart and use on a desktop or on the floor. See Chapters 3 and 7 of *Words Their Way*, 3rd edition (*WTW*) and the *Words Their Way* CD-ROM (*WTWCD*) for additional background information, organizational tips, games, and activities. (References to chapters and pages will be to the 3rd edition. Earlier versions of *WTW* will have different chapter numbering and pages.)

INTRODUCING SORTS

Sorts can be introduced in a number of ways, and the way you choose will depend upon your own teaching style as well as the experience of your students. In *WTW* we describe *teacher-directed sorts, student-centered sorts*, and *Guess My Category* sorts. Most of the sorts in this book are set up for teacher-directed sorts with the categories already established with headers and key words. These sorts work well when you are introducing a new unit or if you feel that your students need more explicit modeling and explanation. However, if you wish to make word sorting into more of a constructive process where students discover the categories, you can cut off the headers before distributing the word sheets and use student-centered sorts as a way to begin. *Guess My Category* sorts also engage the students in more active thinking. Cut off the headers, but use the key words to establish the categories without giving away the feature characteristics of each category. (See *WTW* for more details on different sorting activities).

When you introduce the sorts that include prefixes, suffixes, and base words or word roots/combining forms, you will find the teacher explanations in Chapter 8 of *Words Their Way* to be helpful guides. These scripts provide examples of how to "walk through" the process in which words are formed through this combination of elements.

In addition, many of the sorts provide you with additional information about the etymological derivations of words in the sort. Also information is often provided about processes of language change that have influenced the spelling, pronunciation, and meaning of the words (e.g., why the spelling of some Latin roots changes across related words, as in *scribe* and *script*). Use this information at your discretion to elaborate students' understanding and to provide interesting tidbits to whet their linguistic appetites.

PACING

The pacing for these sorts is designed for average growth. After introducing a sort you should spend about a week working with the words, though quite often you may feel that a sort may lead to two weeks of exploration. This may be especially true of the root sorts. Of course, you may choose to skip some sorts altogether. Although these sorts are arranged in a sequence that builds on earlier understandings, in some cases you may decide to use the sorts out of order. Some of the Greek and Latin word root sorts, for example, can be used earlier than what we present here. In general, this collection of sorts might be considered the spelling/vocabulary curriculum for about a two-year period, with time for extra sorts, when needed, or for review periods. Students' progress through these sorts should be carefully monitored with the goal of building a good foundation for future spelling and vocabulary growth.

STANDARD WEEKLY ROUTINES

1. **Repeated Work with the Words:** Each student should have their own copy of words to cut apart for sorting. We suggest that you enlarge the blackline masters so that no border is left around the words on the sheets that the students receive. This will reduce the amount of waste paper and cutting time. After you have modeled and discussed the sort, students should repeat the sort several times independently. The word cards can be clipped together, or can be stored in an envelope or plastic bag to be sorted again on other days and taken home to sort for homework. Chapter 3 of *WTW* contains tips for managing sorting and homework routines.
2. **Explore Word Meanings with Dictionaries:** From the beginning of these sorts, copies of unabridged dictionaries should be available in the classroom so that students can

explore information about the meaning and origins of words. In addition to these classroom copies, many online dictionaries include this information as well. One source is *The American Heritage Dictionary* at **http://www.yourdictionary.com**. Examples of dictionary use will be suggested throughout this supplement. Unless otherwise noted, definitions used in this supplement are from the *American Heritage Dictionary* (4th Edition). We suggest that students keep dictionaries handy to look up words during the discussion part of lessons. Teachers can use these discussions to teach students features of dictionaries such as pronunciation guides, etymological information, multiple definitions, and so on. We do not recommend assigning students to look up and write out the definitions of more than a selected group of words, as this is not likely to stimulate interest in dictionary use; however, students can be assigned to look up at least one word and report on it to the class.

3. **Teacher Introduction of Unfamiliar Words:** Some words in the sorts may be unfamiliar to the students. When a pair of related words are both unfamiliar, or for any word that is unfamiliar to the students, you have several options for introducing them.

   First, you can wait until after sorting to explore word meanings because the sort itself (especially with words that share common roots) will help students develop hypotheses about meanings that may then be checked in a dictionary. Of course, sometimes you may simply tell students the definition in everyday terms, using the word in the context of an appropriate sentence and discussing it with students.

   Second, you may scaffold or support the students' attempts to determine the meaning in the following format: Construct a one-, two-, or three-sentence context in which the target word occurs, together with two or three scaffolding questions that lead students toward an understanding of the word's meaning. For example, in sort 8 the word pair *allude/allusion* is presented. Students probably do not know either word, so the base word *allude* (meaning to make an indirect reference to something) will be presented as follows:

   > Brent wanted Allison to know that he realized he had acted immaturely when they went to the movie together. He didn't want to refer directly to his flipping popcorn at the screen, so instead he planned to **allude** to it by saying something like "There probably are better ways to impress a date!"

   - Did Brent want to mention the fact that he was flipping popcorn at the screen?
   - How did he decide he would let Allison know he wasn't going to behave like that again?
   - So, what do you think **allude** means?

   A student can check the hypothesized meaning in the dictionary. Because of the suffixation pattern the students are studying, they should be able to infer the meaning of the related word in the sort, *allusion*, from an understanding of the meaning of *allude*.

   As students become familiar with this format, they can take turns each week in looking ahead to the following sort you plan to use, checking the dictionary for definitions of words that are unfamiliar, and constructing their own scaffolding formats. They can then walk their fellow students through their formats.

4. **Writing Sorts and Word Study/Vocabulary Notebooks:** Students should record their word sorts by writing them into columns in their notebooks under the same key words that headed the columns of their word sort. At the bottom of the writing sort, have your students **reflect** on and **declare** what they learned in that particular sort; this is especially important because many of the sorts involve learning rules about the addition of affixes to base words or word roots or learning the meanings of roots and affixes. When there are rules that may be generated, ask them to write these rules in their own words.

   Students may also record new, interesting words they encounter in reading in these notebooks. A separate section, denoted by a tab, may be used to contain these words. (See the procedure for recording new words in Chapter 8 of *Words Their Way*.)

5. **Word Hunts:** Students should look for words that mirror the features studied in the weekly word sorts in their daily reading as well as in other resources. Some features may be rare in daily reading materials, but students can learn to use dictionaries and online resources. Prefixes are particularly easy to find with a dictionary, but students can learn to search by word parts that occur in the middle or at the end of words by going to online resources such as **www.yourdictionary.com** or **www.onelook.com**. At these sites you can type in an asterisk and then a word part to get a list of words (e.g., **cian* for an ending or **bio**).

   Students can also brainstorm together and get ideas from home. Challenge them to find other words that contain the same affixes, bases, or roots. After they find examples they can add the words to the bottom of the proper column in their vocabulary notebooks. You may want to create posters or displays of all the words students discover for each category. Sometimes such group efforts help students make generalizations about the frequency and usefulness of certain rules or features.

6. **No-Peeking or Blind Sorts:** A no-peeking/blind sort should only be done after students have practiced a sort several times, attending to whatever bases, affixes, and/or roots are emphasized. Headers or key words are laid down and students work together in a **buddy sort**. One student calls out a word without showing it. The other student points to where the word should go and the partner then shows the word card to check its spelling against the key word. In a no-peeking/blind **writing sort**, the student writes the word in the proper category, using the key word as a model for spelling. After the word has been written, the partner calling the words shows the word card to the student doing the writing to check for correctness. These sorts require students to think about words by sound and by pattern and to use the key words as models for analogy. Buddy sorts are a great way to practice for spelling tests and can be assigned for homework.

7. **Assessment:** Students can be assessed by asking them to spell the words they have worked with over the week. You could call out only 10 or 15 of the 24 words as a spell check. As you move farther along through the sorts, a larger proportion of the words in a particular sort may be unfamiliar to most students. Unfamiliar words, however, are usually structurally related to known words in the sort, thereby enabling students to infer their probable meanings. As an assessment activity, you can give students a few of these words and ask them to describe an activity, situation, or state of mind in which they use each word. (Examples of this format will occasionally be provided in the context of specific sorts.) *Cumulative Checks* will occur at intervals throughout the supplement. The Cumulative Check assesses students' retention of particular words they have studied in each unit.

SORTS 1-4

Prefixes and Suffixes

NOTES FOR THE TEACHER

Prefixes and suffixes, collectively referred to as *affixes*, are reviewed and extended in these four sorts. The prefixes *un-, re-, dis-, mis-,* and *pre-* were covered in the syllables and affixes stage, but are well worth reviewing at the beginning of the school year. Similarly, the suffixes *-er, -est, -ness, -ful,* and *-less* should be familiar. Some of the words in which these affixes occur, however, are more appropriate for study in higher grades. For example, words such as *murkier/murkiest* and *stodgier/stodgiest* are less familiar or unknown. Other words lend themselves to exploration of more abstract or *metaphorical* meaning, as for example *fruitless*, which can literally mean "without fruit," but has acquired a more metaphorical meaning. The prefixes *fore-, post-,* and *after-*, while familiar to students, are often not examined until this point. For example, familiar words such as *foreword* and *forewarn* need to be examined in light of their component morphemes. The spelling of most of these words may not be particularly challenging, as they are made up of base words that are very familiar and affixes that are spelled regularly; however, working with the sorts helps students think through the generative process of how word elements—affixes and bases—are put together.

There are many ways in which students can examine the prefix/suffix plus base word process. Other sorts are suggested in *WTW* and on the *WTWCD*. Word hunts will be especially fruitful when students look for words that contain the affixes shown in these sorts. The dictionary is an easy place to hunt for words with prefixes, but students should avoid selecting words such as *reason, mistress,* or *precious* that do not have true prefixes. At this point students should hunt for words in which a recognizable word part remains when the prefix is removed.

SORT 1   REVIEW OF PREFIXES (UN-, RE-, DIS-, MIS-)

This sort discusses the prefixes *un-*, which means "not"; *re-*, which means "again" or "back"; *dis-*, which means "not" or "undo"; and *mis-*, which means "bad" or "badly."

Demonstrate

Prepare a set of words to use for teacher-directed modeling. Save the discussion of word meanings until after sorting. Display a transparency of the words on the overhead or hand out the sheet of words to the students. Ask them what they notice about the words and get ideas about how the words can be sorted. Students usually notice that all the words contain prefixes. Remind them of the term **base word**, which applies to the word to which prefixes and suffixes are added. Put up the headers and key words and then sort the rest of the words.

The discussion after the first sort might go something like this: "Look at the words under *un-*. What do you notice about the meanings of these words?" Focus on the key word *unopened*. Ask students for the base word. Explain that a **prefix** has been added to the base word and that it changes the meaning of the word. Ask students what *unopened* means (something that is not opened, such as a letter or a package). Repeat this with the next three words under *un-*, talking about the meaning of each word. Then remind students that a prefix has a meaning of its own and ask them what *un-* means in the first four words (it means "not" or "the opposite of"). Repeat this with the words under *re-*, *dis-*, and *mis-* to review the meaning of each prefix: *Re-* means "to do again," but also means more like "back" in *reaction*; *dis-* usually means "not"; *mis-* means to do something "badly." Ask students if they've thought about how *disease* can literally mean "the opposite of" *ease*? Do they see how *mistake* literally means "take badly"? You might also talk about how the word *misstep* is often misspelled (like *misspelled*) with an *s* left out. Ask students why there must be two *ss*—one goes with the prefix and the other with the base word.

un-	re-	dis-	mis-
unopened	**repackage**	**discontinue**	**misfortune**
unread	reinstall	distrust	mislead
unheated	reconsider	disorder	misconduct
unattached	reaction	disengage	misplace
unplanned	reform	disease	misstep
unglued	reassure	disclose	mistake

Extend

Students can go on *word hunts* to locate as many words as they can with these prefixes. There will be some "exceptions"; that is, words such as *uncle* and *reach* that do not have identifiable prefixes because there is no base word left when the prefix is removed. They are likely to find many words that consist of a familiar prefix and a word that does not stand by itself, such as *rebellion*. Without the prefix we are left with the root *bellion*, which does not have a familiar meaning. These roots will be examined later on in the derivational relations stage, and you may decide to explain the difference between base words and word roots to the students. Students can look up any words that they don't know the meaning of or that they have questions about. For example, the word *rebellion* actually contains the prefix *re-* and the word root *-bel-*, which comes from a Latin word that means "war." *Rebellion* (and *rebel*) literally mean "to war against." Word roots are word parts that come from Greek and Latin and do not stand alone as base words. This mentioning of word roots and how they function within words will plant the seed for more extensive exploration of these important elements later on. (For example, in sort 30 the words *antebellum* and *postbellum* are examined.)

SORT 2   PREFIXES (*PRE-, FORE-, POST-, AFTER-*)
Demonstrate

Have students sort the words according to their prefixes. Then, have them discuss how *prewar* and *postwar* are alike and different; do the same for the other word pairs, *preseason/postseason* and *predate/postdate*. The word *prefix* offers an excellent opportunity for thinking explicitly about what this term means; literally, "to fix before." Compare and contrast *forethought/afterthought* and *foreword/afterword.* The latter word pair may be illustrated by showing the students a book that has a foreword and an after-word. A *foreword* is usually written by someone other than the author. If the word *preface* does not come up in this discussion, you may choose to mention it: It literally means "to speak before" and, in contrast to a foreword, is usually written by the author. *Preexisting*, by the way, offers another opportunity to look at the rationale under-lying double letters. Ask students why there are two *e*'s in the word *preexisting*

pre-	fore-	post-	after-
prewar	**forethought**	**postwar**	**afterthought**
prejudge	foreword	postcolonial	afterword
preseason	forearm	postseason	afternoon
predate	forecourt	postdate	aftertaste
preoccupied	foreknowledge		
preposition	foreordain		
predetermine	forewarn		
prefix			
preexisting			

Extend

The game *Prefix Spin* described in Chapter 7 of WTW may be adapted to review the prefixes presented in these first two sorts (*un-, re-, dis-,* and *mis-,* and *pre-, fore-, post-, and after-*). Students will be able to see how the same base words and prefixes can be used in many different combinations to form words with meanings that they can understand. The base word *form,* for example, can be used to form *misform, reform, preform.*

SORT 3 REVIEW OF COMPARATIVE SUFFIXES (-ER, -EST, -IER, -IEST)

Demonstrate

Introduce this sort in a manner similar to sort 1, reviewing the term **suffix**. Sort first by *-er* and *-est* and talk about the meaning of the words and what the suffix does to the base word. (When comparing two things, *-er* is used. When comparing more than two things, use *-est.*) Ask students to underline the base words to highlight the fact that the base word in *emptier* or *emptiest* has been changed. Sort these words into two new categories under *-ier* and *-iest.* Ask the students to form a generalization that covers these words (e.g., when a word ends in *y*, change the *y* to *i* before adding the suffix).

-er	-est	-ier	-iest
kinder	**kindest**	**emptier**	**emptiest**
stranger	strangest	earlier	earliest
cleaner	cleanest	trickier	trickiest
quieter	quietest	fancier	fanciest
harsher	harshest	crummier	crummiest
		murkier	murkiest
		shinier	shiniest

Extend

To review the rules involved in adding suffixes, sort the words as shown below:

e-drop	Change y to i	Nothing
stranger	emptier	cleaner
strangest	earlier	cleanest
	trickier	quieter
	trickiest	quietest
	fancier	harsher
	fanciest	harshest
	crummier	
	crummiest	
	murkier	
	murkiest	
	shinier	
	shiniest	

To help students **transfer** their understanding of these rules to new words, ask them to add -*er* and -*est* to these words: *dense, deadly, sunny, sweet, loud, hungry.*

SORT 4   REVIEW OF SUFFIXES (-*NESS*, -*FUL*, -*LESS*)

Demonstrate

Students should be able to do this as a student-centered sort and establish the categories for themselves. Discuss with students how the suffixes change the meaning and use of the word. The suffix -*ness* creates nouns out of adjectives and suggests a "state of being." The suffixes -*ful* and -*less* create adjectives that mean "full of" or "having," and "without." The word *priceless* is interesting; literally, it means "without price" and students may ask whether it means something that is so worthless or cheap that it literally has no price. Theoretically it could, of course; but the meaning of the word *priceless* has evolved over the years to mean something that is so incredibly valuable that you could not put a price on it.

Draw students' attention to the base words and ask them to find any that have been changed before adding these suffixes. They should see that words ending in a consonant or *e* simply add the endings that start with consonants and do not require any such changes. Base words that end in *y*, however, must change the *y* to *i* (*friendliness, emptiness, bountiful, fanciful*).

-*ness*	-*ful*	-*less*	Combination of suffixes
looseness	**delightful**	**breathless**	**thoughtlessness**
massiveness	disgraceful	scoreless	tactlessness
attentiveness	bountiful	thoughtless	flawlessness
politeness	insightful	priceless	
friendliness	fanciful	flawless	
emptiness	tactful	tactless	
rigorousness	respectful	fruitless	

Extend

Challenge students to create even more combination words from the other words in the sort: *disgraceful/disgracefulness, insightful/insightfulness, humorless/humorlessness*, and so forth.

CUMULATIVE CHECK 1

Ask students to spell and define the following words:

1. misconduct
2. respectful
3. disengage
4. unattached
5. preoccupied
6. breathless
7. friendliness
8. disorder
9. preoccupied
10. attentiveness
11. murkier
12. fruitless
13. tactlessness
14. preexisting
15. rigorousness

SORT 1 Review of Prefixes (un-, re-, dis-, mis-)

un-	re-	dis-	mis-
unopened	**repackage**	**discontinue**	
mislead	reinstall	**misfortune**	
distrust	reaction	unheated	
reconsider	disorder	misconduct	
unread	mistake	unattached	
disengage	misplace	misstep	
reform	disease	unplanned	
unglued	reassure	disclose	

SORT 2   Prefixes (pre-, fore-, post-, after-)

pre-	fore-	post-	after-
prewar	**postwar**	**forethought**	
afterword	foreword	**afterthought**	
preseason	forearm	postcolonial	
afternoon	predate	preoccupied	
postseason	prejudge	preposition	
postdate	forecourt	predetermine	
foreordain	prefix	foreknowledge	
forewarn	aftertaste	preexisting	

Words Their Way: Word Sorts for Derivational Relations Spellers © 2006 by Prentice-Hall, Inc.

SORT 3   Review of Comparative Suffixes (-er, -est, -ier, -iest)

-er	-est	-ier	-iest
kinder	**kindest**	**emptier**	
emptiest	stranger	cleaner	
earlier	quietest	trickier	
fanciest	crummier	strangest	
cleanest	quieter	earliest	
trickiest	murkiest	harsher	
crummiest	harshest	shinier	
fancier	shiniest	murkier	

Words Their Way: Word Sorts for Derivational Relations Spellers © 2006 by Prentice-Hall, Inc.

SORT 4 Review of Suffixes (-ness, -ful, -less)

-ness	-ful	-less	combination
looseness	**delightful**	**breathless**	
emptiness	bountiful	**thoughtlessness**	
disgraceful	fanciful	tactlessness	
politeness	fruitless	friendliness	
respectful	priceless	flawlessness	
thoughtless	flawless	attentiveness	
scoreless	tactful	rigorousness	
insightful	tactless	massiveness	

SORTS 5-8

Spelling-Meaning Patterns I

NOTES FOR THE TEACHER

The suffix /shun/, as in *nation, session, musician,* can be spelled several ways (*-ion, -tion, -sion, -ian*) and this poses a challenge for spellers. When added to a base, *-ion* often has the effect of "softening" the final consonant sound, as in *select/selection* (a consequence that often leads to spelling confusions).

The generalizations that govern which affix to add and how to add it are reliable but complex and are covered in a series of sorts in this unit. Hundreds of words end with *-ion,* so spending an extended time with this suffix is worthwhile. If you desire you can break this unit into two or three parts and revisit the sorts rather than going through all of them sequentially.

You may wish to share with the students that the suffix *-ion* occurs with considerable frequency and refers to an "action or process" or "the *result* of an action or process" (e.g., if you have an *attraction* for someone, you are *attracted* toward them). Another way to think about it is that adding *-ion* to a word usually changes it from a verb (*decorate*) to a noun (*decoration*). The suffix *-ian* is added to nouns and often suggests someone who "does" (*musician*).

The generalizations that govern how to add *-ion* are complex because they depend upon how the base word ends. You may want to create a chart that you add to with each new sort, but students are likely to develop a "feel" for these generalizations and there is no reason to expect them to memorize the various conditions. We will list them here for your information:

Base words that end in two consonants just add *-ion* (*subtraction, expression*).
Base words that end in *ic* add *-ian* (*magician*).
Base words that end in *te* drop the *e* and add *-ion* (*creation*).
Base words that end in *de* and *it* drop those letters and add *-sion* or *-ssion* (*explode* to *explosion, admit* to *admission*).
Base words that end in *ce* drop the *e* and add a *t* to change the soft *c* (*produce*) to a hard *c* (*production*).

SORT 5   ADDING *-ION* TO BASE WORDS, NO SPELLING CHANGE

Demonstrate

Display a transparency of the words on the overhead or hand out the sheet of words to the students. Ask them what they notice about the words and get ideas about how the words can be sorted. Students usually note that some of the words have familiar prefixes such as those covered in the last unit and many end in *-ion*. Tell them that they will be examining the suffix *-ion* and what happens when it is added to base words. Put up the headers and key words and then sort the rest of the words. Begin by sorting the base words by the final letters (*ct* and *ss*) under the headers. Then match the affixed word to the base.

The discussion after the sort might go something like this: "Pronounce the words under *subtraction*. What do you notice about how the base word changes when *-ion* is added?" (The final /t/ sound changes to the sound of /sh/.) "Now, pronounce the words under *expression*. What do you notice about these words when *-ion* is added?" (The final /s/ sound also becomes the sound of /sh/.) Make sure that students understand that there is no change in the spelling of the base word when adding *-ion* to base words that end in *ct* or *ss*. Next, discuss the first few base words under *subtract* and *express*: Beginning with *subtract*, ask the students what the base word means and then ask them what the suffixed word means. Encourage them to put the meanings into their own words. What happens when we put *-ion* onto a base word? Scaffold their understandings of the following: Putting *-ion* on a base word results in a word that means "the act or result" of the meaning of the base word. For example, if you *predict* that a team will win a game you have made a *prediction*; the act of subtracting one number from another is called the process of *subtraction*.

In discussing *detect* and *detection*, ask the students what other word that they know very well is in this same spelling-meaning family (*detective*).

Base -*ct*	*ct* + *ion*	Base -*ss*	*ss* + *ion*
subtract	**subtraction**	**express**	**expression**
distinct	distinction	oppress	oppression
elect	election	possess	possession
predict	prediction	profess	profession
extinct	extinction	congress	congressional
detect	detection	confess	confession

If students do not readily arrive at the generalization about adding *-ion* to words of these types, then have them arrange the words vertically by placing the suffixed words underneath the base word. Then, examine the spelling correspondence across words.

Extend

When students go on word hunts they will find many words that end with *-ion* that do not fit either the *ct* or the *ss* category. At this point help the students identify words that come from base words that end in either *ct* or *ss* and have them add those to their word study notebooks. Other words ending in *-tion* will go into the miscellaneous category for now. Students can refer to their lists as they add more categories in the sorts that follow and put those words into the appropriate categories.

SORT 6   ADDING -ION AND -IAN, NO SPELLING CHANGE

Demonstrate

Introduce this sort in the same manner as sort 5. You may need to discuss the words *optic* and *logician*. After the students have noted the base word/suffixed word distinction, discuss the base + -ion pattern, examining the suffix -ion and what happens to the sound of *t* when it is added to the base words. Then, have students examine the base word + -ian pattern and how the sound of the *c* changes. Facilitate their discussion of how -ian is different from -ion: -ian usually refers to a person who does something, as in *magician* (more broadly, "relating to, belonging to, or resembling"; this pattern will be revisited in sort 16). Next, examine the base words that end in *t*. Remind the students that last week they looked at words ending in *ct*. Ask them what they notice about these words (they also end in a consonant +*t* and simply add -ion). Note that sometimes words ending in two consonants add -ation, as in *adaptation* and *condemnation*. These are easy to spell because we can clearly hear the "ation."

Base -t	Base + ion	Base -ic	Base + ian
assert	**assertion**	**magic**	**magician**
digest	digestion	music	musician
invent	invention	optic	optician
suggest	suggestion	logic	logician
adopt	adoption	diagnostic	diagnostician
insert	insertion	clinic	clinician

In spelling, the treatment of -ion is a confusion common primarily at the syllables and affixes stage, but also at the derivational relations stage. Students often remember the various spellings (-ion, -tion, -sion, -ation), but are uncertain about when to use a particular spelling, and whether and how it affects the spelling of the base word. These orthographic conditions, examined in sorts 5 and 6, are examined in sorts 7 and 8 in this cycle as well. Subsequent sorts will revisit this feature as appropriate.

When students are uncertain about whether the spelling is -ion or -ian, the "default" spelling is usually -ion. The meaning of -ian, however, is different than that of the orthographically similar -ion. In terms of *sound*, the effect of -ian on the base word to which it is attached is the same as that of -ion: It "softens" the consonant sound at the end of the base (*music/musician*).

SORT 7   ADDING -ION, E-DROP AND SPELLING CHANGE

Demonstrate

Have the students sort the words so that each base matches up with its suffixed or derived word. Then ask the students if they see another way in which the base words and suffixed words can be sorted. If necessary, mention that, just as with the words in the previous sort, they should pay attention to whether the sound of the base word changes when a suffix is added. Discuss how, in addition to dropping the *e* in the -uce words, a *t* must be added to -ion. If the students want to pursue the reason for this, you might ask them how the suffixed word would be spelled if the *t* were not added (e.g., *producion*).

How might it be pronounced? (Perhaps something like "proDOOshun.") Share with the students that English has evolved such that there's no such spelling or pronunciation. The *t* was added to *-ion* to keep the hard sound of the *c*.

You may wish to ask the students if they see a base word within *decorate*. Ask them if they've heard of the word *décor* before. Discuss its meaning.

Base -*te*	e-drop + *ion*	Base -*ce*	e-drop + *tion*
congratulate	**congratulation**	**produce**	**production**
create	creation	introduce	introduction
decorate	decoration	reduce	reduction
generate	generation	reproduce	reproduction
imitate	imitation		
illustrate	illustration		
indicate	indication		
translate	translation		

Extend

When students go on word hunts they now have five categories of base words to consider when they come across words that end in *-ion*. Although not many words end in *ce* and add *-ction*, students should find lots that drop the *e*. When students find words in which the spelling of the base changes when the suffix is added, have them record these words in a "miscellaneous" category, but ask them to keep their eyes open for a pattern in these words as well. (These patterns are explored later in sorts 28 and 38.)

SORT 8   ADDING -*ION*: PREDICTABLE CHANGES IN CONSONANTS

Demonstrate

Have the students sort the base words into two categories. They will probably notice that the words have different endings: Some end in *de* and others end in *t*. Next, have the students match each base word with its suffixed form. Ask them what happens when *-ion* is added to the "explode" group? What happens when *-ion* is added to the "admit" group? Have them record these sorts in their vocabulary notebooks and write a "rule" in their own words. When adding *-ion* to words that end in *de*, drop the *de* and add *-sion*. When adding *-ion* to words that end in *i* + *t*, drop the *t* and add *ss*.

Base -*de*	-*de* > *sion*	Base -*it*	-*it* > *ission*
explode	**explosion**	**admit**	**admission**
decide	decision	omit	omission
divide	division	permit	permission
invade	invasion	submit	submission
conclude	conclusion		
intrude	intrusion		
protrude	protrusion		
allude	allusion		

Extend

Remind students that they have studied other word pairs in which the suffixed word has a double *ss* before *-ion* (e.g., *confess/confession* and *profess/profession*). When they find such words in their word hunts they will have to consider the spelling of the base word before assigning them to categories. Not many words fall into the category of changing *it* to *ssion*, but they are formed with a high degree of regularity. A few more include *commission, emission, remission,* and *transmission.*

CUMULATIVE CHECK 2

Review and Transfer

Write the following previously studied base words on the board: *profess, create, infect, music, decide, introduce,* and *permit.* Have students explain the spelling change that occurs when /shun/ is added to each one. Now write the new base words below and ask students to spell the words in parentheses as you pronounce them.

1. discuss (discussion)	2. donate (donation)	3. electric (electrician)
4. object (objection)	5. collide (collision)	6. deduce (deduction)
7. transmit (transmission)	8. correct (correction)	9. pediatric (pediatrician)
10. invade (invasion)	11. locate (location)	12. impress (impression)

Assessment

Call out the first eight words in the following list to check for retention of the words covered in the sorts. Call out the last four words to test for transfer of the generalizations. Be ready to tell students the base word. To check definitional understanding of some of the words, you may wish to have the students write sentences using them.

1. election	2. possession	3. musician
4. generation	5. reduction	6. decision
7. permission	8. illustration	9. location
10. erosion	11. objection	12. depression

SORT 5   Adding *-ion* to Base Words, No Spelling Change

base *-ct*	*-ct* + *ion*	base *-ss*	*-ss* + *ion*
subtract	**subtraction**	**express**	
distinct	**expression**	oppress	
elect	distinction	predict	
detection	oppression	election	
possess	confession	extinction	
profess	congressional	possession	
prediction	profession	detect	
extinct	congress	confess	

Words Their Way: Word Sorts for Derivational Relations Spellers © 2006 by Prentice-Hall, Inc.

SORT 6   Adding *-ion* and *-ian*, No Spelling Change

base *-t*	+ *ion*	base *-ic*	+ *ian*
assert	**assertion**		**magic**
magician	invention		digest
music	suggestion		optic
optician	digestion		invent
clinic	adoption		musician
diagnostic	logician		suggest
adopt	insertion		logic
insert	diagnostician		clinician

Words Their Way: Word Sorts for Derivational Relations Spellers © 2006 by Prentice-Hall, Inc.

base *-te*	e-drop + *ion*	base *-ce*	e-drop + *tion*
congratulate	congratulation		produce
production	decoration		create
reduction	introduction		reduce
illustrate	reproduction		creation
imitation	generation		indicate
reproduce	indication		decorate
introduce	illustration		generate
imitate	translation		translate

SORT 8 Adding -ion: Predictable Changes in Consonants

base -de	sion	base -it	ission
explode	**explosion**		**admit**
admission	decide		invasion
omit	permission		submit
decision	conclusion		omission
protrude	invade		intrude
submission	protrusion		permit
intrusion	conclude		division
allude	divide		allusion

Words Their Way: Word Sorts for Derivational Relations Spellers © 2006 by Prentice-Hall, Inc.

SORTS 9–19

Spelling-Meaning Patterns II

NOTES FOR THE TEACHER

Beginning with sorts 9–19, students will explicitly explore the spelling-meaning connection through the examination of vowel and consonant *alternations*. The term *alternation* refers to the sound changes that occur across words that are related in spelling and meaning. In sort 9, for example, the silent consonant in one word in a spelling/meaning pair is sounded in the related word (*sign/signature*); in sort 10, the long vowel in one word alternates with a short vowel in the related word (*nature/natural*). The *spelling*, however, changes little if at all—and this is the essence of the *spelling-meaning connection*: **Words that are related in meaning are often related in spelling as well, despite changes in sound.** Students' understanding of this connection is an important strategy: When uncertain how to spell a particular word, students should try to think of another word that is related in terms of spelling and meaning, and it will usually provide a clue. As we will see in later sorts, the *spelling-meaning connection* also supports vocabulary development: If students understand one word in a spelling-meaning family of words, they usually can learn the meanings of the related words. The similar spelling of words in a spelling-meaning family visually represents the meaning relationships that they share.

You may find it helpful to develop a system for marking vowels and stress as you work with these words to draw attention to the way sounds and stress alternate in pairs of words. Vowels may be marked as long (macron) or short (breve) or with a schwa. Stressed syllables might be marked with accent marks or be underlined.

Students may have difficulty finding more pairs of words with consonant and vowel alternations since these are often not obvious until the two words are side by side.

SORT 9   SILENT/SOUNDED CONSONANT ALTERNATION

This sort provides an excellent opportunity to introduce students explicitly to the relationship between spelling and meaning.

Demonstrate

You may introduce the sort by saying to the students, as you write on the board, "When I *sign* my name [write *sign* on the board] I include a *g* even though I do not hear it. I've just given you a clue as to *why* there's a *g* in the word *sign*." If the students do not respond, prompt them with "When you sign a letter, what is that called?" [*Signature*] "Do you hear the sound of the *g* now?" Underline the *g* in both words. Follow this up by writing *muscle* on the board. "What letter is silent in this word? Is there a word related in spelling and meaning to *muscle* and in which the *c* is pronounced?" [*Muscular*] Write *muscular* underneath *muscle* and underline the *c* in both words. Explain to the students that words related in meaning are often related in spelling as well, despite changes in sound. Thinking of a related word may help students remember how to spell another word.

Set up *sign* and *signature* as headers and model how to sort two or three more pairs of words. Ask students which pair has a silent letter and place it under *sign*. Continue sorting all of the words with the students' help.

Silent Consonant	Sounded Consonant
sign	**signature**
bomb	bombard
soften	soft
muscle	muscular
condemn	condemnation
design	designate
column	columnist
autumn	autumnal
resign	resignation
hasten	haste
solemn	solemnity
moisten	moist

The meaning or connection between most of the words in this sort is fairly straightforward. Sometimes, however, this relationship is not as apparent—as, for example, between *design* and *designate*. This is a good opportunity to refer students to the etymological information for *design* and *designate* in the dictionary; both words come from a Latin term that means "to mark." When someone is *designated* as a spokesperson, for example, she or he is in a sense "marked" to perform this duty. When an architect *designs* a house, she is "marking" how the house will be laid out and how it will look.

Extend

The words in this sort offer possibilities for suffix exploration. The suffix *-ion* has already been explored in sorts 5, 6, 7, and 8. You can ask the students to identify other suffixes in the derived words and suggest their meanings and/or their effects on the base to which they are attached. In *condemnation* and *resignation* an *a* has been added before the *-tion* ending. Speculate about why this is so and look for a pattern. (The base word ends in the letter *n*, so now there is another category of base words to add to the chart!)

SORT 10   VOWEL ALTERNATION: LONG TO SHORT

Sort 10 focuses on the constancy of spelling despite a change in pronunciation of the vowel from the base to its derived word or its *derivative*, a word that comes from or is *derived* from the base. (This is an appropriate place in word study at the derivational level to begin to use this term.)

Demonstrate

Ask the students how they might sort the words. They will probably notice that some are base words. Suggest that they sort the words into base words and related suffixed or *derived* words. *Grateful/gratitude* and *breath/breathe* present opportunities for discussion (e.g., is *grate* a word? Actually, it was in Middle English, as an unabridged dictionary will reveal.). As for *breath* and *breathe,* both words look like a base. (Is *breathe* a "suffixed" word?) If they do not notice this, mention that the word *mine* refers to a place in which minerals are extracted or dug out. After the related words have been matched up, ask the students if the vowel sounds in the accented syllables of the word pairs change. (Yes, they do.) Does the spelling of the vowel change? (No.) Remind the students that this is because the words are related in meaning; this is the *spelling-meaning connection.*

Because the primary focus here is on the spelling-meaning connection, it is not necessary to address the effect that the several different suffixes exert on each base. You may feel, however, that some students might benefit from a brief "mentioning" or discussion of this effect; for example, you could point out how *-al* ("of or relating to") affects the base words *nature, nation, crime.*

Long Vowel	Short Vowel
type	**typical**
mine	mineral
breathe	breath
revise	revision
nature	natural
nation	national
athlete	athletic
grateful	gratitude
crime	criminal
humane	humanity
ignite	ignition
precise	precision

SORT 11   VOWEL ALTERNATION: LONG TO SHORT/SCHWA

The words in this sort help students contrast the long/short vowel alternation pattern with a schwa. Many spelling errors at this level are in the unaccented syllables of words, so these spelling-meaning patterns are helpful to study. Importantly, this sort will help students attend to accent within words.

Introduce the sort by asking the students if they've ever had to stop and think about how to spell a particular word, such as *competition* or *admiration*? Tell them that thinking of a related word may provide a clue. For example, thinking of the base word *compete* will help with spelling the word *competition*; thinking of the base word *admire* may help with *admiration.* Tell them that this is one of the spelling/meaning patterns they are going to explore in these words.

Have the students match up each base word with its derivative. If they do not notice the different type of vowel alternation on their own, ask them to compare the pair *volcano/volcanic* with *compose/composition.* In *volcano/volcanic,* do they hear how the long *a* in *volcano* changes to a short *a* in *volcanic*? Does the long *o* in *composition* change to a short *o* in *composition*? Not exactly. In *volcanic,* is the second syllable clearly accented—in other words, does it get most of the "oomph" when we say the word? In *composition,* is the second syllable clearly accented? Not really. Because the second syllable is not accented, the vowel sound in the second syllable of *composition* sounds like a schwa, an unaccented short *-u* sound, because there's no "oomph" behind it. Have students look up several of the derived words to see how the schwa is represented in their dictionary.

The students may note that they can clearly hear the vowel sound in the second syllable of *reptile* even though it is not accented. Yes, this type of alternation does occur in many words, but in most unaccented or least accented syllables the vowel sound is also unaccented, becoming a schwa.

Students may begin to notice and comment on relationships that do not appear to make sense in terms of spelling and meaning. For example, are *admiral* and *admire* related? These words actually come from different languages and are not related in meaning. *Admire* comes from French in which it means "to wonder" (and is related to *miracle* and *miraculous*, which also have to do with "wonder"); *admiral* comes from an Arabic word for "commander." Occasionally, exceptions such as these do occur. Exploring the history or etymology of the terms usually reveals the disconnect.

Base Word: Long Vowel	Base Word: Short Vowel	Base Word: Long Vowel	Base Word: Schwa
volcano	volcanic	compose	composition
reptile	reptilian	compete	competition
rite	ritual	admire	admiration
divine	divinity	custodian	custody
serene	serenity	define	definition
conspire	conspiracy		
page	paginate		

Discuss how *custodian* refers not just to an individual who maintains the condition of a school; it has a broader application, referring to anyone who holds custody of something, including an idea—as, for example, when a people are referred to as "*custodians* of democracy."

SORT 12   ADDING SUFFIXES: VOWEL ALTERNATION, ACCENTED TO UNACCENTED

This sort continues students' exploration of how vowel sounds may alternate across related words, but the spelling remains constant. Students' examination of this type of pattern is very productive because it continues to build a spelling-meaning strategy: If you are uncertain about the spelling of a particular word, thinking of a related word may provide a clue.

Demonstrate

Have students match up each base word with its derived word. Using *similar* and *similarity* as examples, discuss how accent affects each word. In *similar*, is the last syllable accented? (No.) What happens to that syllable when the suffix *-ity* is added? (It becomes accented or stressed.) If students are uncertain about the spelling of the /er/ syllable at the end of *similar*, thinking of the word *similarity* might help them because they can clearly hear the vowel sound in the third syllable of *similarity* and they know how to spell that sound. Because words that are related in spelling are often related in meaning as well, the stressed syllable in *similarity* provides a clue to the spelling of the schwa sound in *similar*.

Discuss one or two other word pairs in the same manner. You may also present a misspelling (*oppisition*, for example) and ask students what word would clear up the spelling of the schwa sound, and why. It may be helpful to mark the stressed syllables with an accent mark or by underlining. Ask students to look up several words to see how stress is marked in their dictionaries.

Base Word	Derived Word
similar	**similarity**
familiar	familiarity
fragile	fragility
combine	combination
invite	invitation
legal	legality
metal	metallic
mobile	mobility
oppose	opposition
perspire	perspiration
preside	president
prohibit	prohibition

SORT 13   ADDING SUFFIX -*ITY*: VOWEL ALTERNATION, SCHWA TO SHORT

Students first dealt with -*ity* in sort 12 and discussed its effect on the pronunciation of the word to which it is affixed. The derivational suffix -*ity* (meaning "state" or "quality") is very common, and for that reason this sort further examines its effect on words. In this sort, the unaccented final syllable in each base word, /al/, becomes accented when -*ity* is affixed.

Demonstrate

Ask the students how they might sort the words. An obvious suggestion is to put the -*ity* words together in one column and their related words in the other column. Ask the students to look at the first few word pairs. What do they notice when -*ity* is added? If they do not mention that they worked with words that end in -*ity* in an earlier sort, remind them of this and mention some of those word pairs (e.g., *legal/legality*, *similar/similarity*).

Schwa	Accented
moral	**morality**
mental	mentality
individual	individuality
general	generality
brutal	brutality
central	centrality
eventual	eventuality
personal	personality
musical	musicality
neutral	neutrality
original	originality
normal	normality

Extend

Ask the students if they have ever heard someone described as having a *genial* personality. How might *genial* be spelled? If they are uncertain—or even if they aren't—ask the students to listen to the following description to see if it provides a clue: "Suzette has a *genial* personality. She is outgoing and supportive, and always wants to know if there is anything she can do for you. Suzette's *geniality* is the most likable aspect of her." Knowing that the vowel sound in the derived word *geniality* is clearly short will help the student know that the unaccented, and therefore ambiguous final syllable in *genial* is spelled with *-al*.

Students should be able to find lots of words that end in *-ity* on a word hunt, although some of them, unlike the words in this sort, will not end in *-lity*.

SORT 14   ADDING SUFFIXES: MULTIPLE VOWEL ALTERNATIONS

Demonstrate

Remind students that they have explored *-ian* before (sort 6). For example, the word *musician* illustrates one of the meanings of *-ian*: "one relating to, belonging to, or resembling" music. Does *-ian* have that meaning in any of the words in this sort? What about *Oregonian*? Discuss how the meaning for *-ian*, "of, relating to, or resembling," fits in.

This sort presents several opportunities for extending students' vocabulary by having the students sort the words into base words and derived words. Students will be familiar with *sufficient*, but may not know *suffice*. Have the students discuss what *sufficient* means, giving examples. Based on the meaning of *sufficient*, therefore, what might *suffice* mean? Both *impede* and *impediment* are probably new terms, so scaffold students' understanding with examples that follow the guidelines in "Teacher Introduction of Unfamiliar Words" (page 4). Discuss with students how a number of words, most often names, such as *Oregon* and *Jefferson*, form adjectives by adding *-ian*. Note that in some word pairs the accented vowel is long (*impose/imposition*); in others, it is short (*specific/specify*). In some word pairs the accented vowel is in the base word (*mediocre*); in others, it is in the derived word (*humidity*). (Note: Dictionaries don't always agree on pronunciation. This is particularly true with respect to unaccented syllables. For example, the *American Heritage Dictionary* lists the boldfaced vowel in *humid* as a short *-i*; *Merriam-Webster* lists it as a schwa.)

Base Word	Derived Word
impose	**imposition**
suffice	sufficient
mediocre	mediocrity
humid	humidity
Palestine	Palestinian
Iran	Iranian
Oregon	Oregonian
Jefferson	Jeffersonian
impede	impediment
ferocious	ferocity
specify	specific
precocious	precocity

Extend

You may wish to have the students do a "part of speech" sort with these words. Students may then be on the lookout, for example, for additional adjectives that are formed by adding *-ian* to a base, and enter these in their vocabulary notebooks.

SORT 15   VOWEL ALTERNATION: ACCENTED TO UNACCENTED

As with previous sorts, this sort continues students' exploration of how vowel sounds may alternate across related words, but the spelling remains constant. Students' examination of this type of pattern is very productive because it continues to build a spelling-meaning strategy: If you are uncertain about the spelling of a particular word, thinking of a related word may provide a clue.

Demonstrate

Have students match up each base word with its derived word. Then have them sort the *word pairs* into the following two categories: Those in which the accent within a pair changes when the suffix is added, and those in which the accent does not change. Some of the word pairs will provide opportunities for expanding vocabulary; be sure to engage the students in discussion about them, encouraging them to think of the meaning of the known word in the word pair as a clue to the meaning of the unfamiliar term. Note that students may be familiar with *harmony* only in terms of music, for example, and not in terms of relationships among people.

Change in Accent		No Change in Accent	
comedy	**comedian**	**narrate**	**narrative**
harmony	harmonious	mandate	mandatory
history	historian		
emphasis	emphatic		
labor	laborious		
rigid	rigidity		
illustrate	illustrative		
tutor	tutorial		
janitor	janitorial		
major	majority		

Students may note that more than one type of sound change is going on between word pairs; for example, *labor* and *laborious*; *major* and *majority*.

SORT 16   ADDING SUFFIXES: VOWEL ALTERNATION, SPELLING CHANGE

This sort examines words in which the spelling of the vowel pattern within the base changes when a suffix is added. Note that, although this change in spelling is an exception to the spelling-meaning connection, it is an exception that nonetheless follows a pattern; that is, when spelling *does* change within a spelling-meaning family of words, it does so *predictably*. There is a *pattern*, in other words, that occurs across words of a certain type, and a number of words usually follow this pattern. Point out to students that, in addition to the *assume/assumption* words in this sort, only one other pair of words follows this pattern: *subsume* and *subsumption*. (Note: The reason for this spelling change is addressed in sorts 28 and 38.)

Demonstrate

Have students sort the words by matching up base words with derived words. After discussing the meanings of any unfamiliar words, students can check the definitions in the dictionary. You may also wish to tell the students that, although there are only a few instances of this particular pattern, you are addressing it to point out that, even when words appear odd, there are almost always other words that follow that same pattern.

Students may not realize that the words *conceive* and *conception* are related to *concept*. Point this out to them and encourage discussion of how these three words or ideas are related to one another. Many students will struggle with the spelling of *conceive* and *receive* because of the unusual *ei* pattern. This may be a good place to review the jingle "*i* before *e* except after *c*." Brainstorm other words that work like this, such as *ceiling*.

Base *-m*	Derived *-ation*	Base *-e*	Derived *-ption*	
exclaim	**exclamation**	**assume**	**assumption**	
proclaim	proclamation	presume	presumption	presumptive
acclaim	acclamation	consume	consumption	
explain	explanation	resume	resumption	
reclaim	reclamation	receive	reception	receptive
		conceive	conception	

SORT 17   ADDING SUFFIXES: OTHER CONSONANT ALTERNATIONS

This sort addresses a particular class of spelling uncertainties among students at this level—the sounds and spellings of *c*, *s*, and *ch*. They will learn, for example, whether *criticize* or *critisize* is correct, or *polititian* or *politician*.

Background Information

You may wish to point out that *politics*, *political*, and *politician* come from the Greek word *polis*, which means "city." In classical Greece, the *city* was the primary form of government, not the nation or country.

Demonstrate

In introducing the sort, ask students to sort together those words that they believe belong together rather than asking them to arrange words into base words and derived words. (This is because in some groupings, such as *physics*/*physicist*, there doesn't appear to be a base word—*physics* without the *s* does not really work here!) Have students examine their groupings, and ask them what they notice. Move them toward the understanding that, although the sound that the letter *c* represents changes within each group, the spelling does not change. Facilitate the students' discussion of what *cosmetician* and *toxicity* might mean. The word *artifice* is more challenging. You might provide context sentences to support students' inferring its meaning, given their knowledge of the meaning of *artificial*.

Base Word: /k/	Derived Word: /s/	Base Word: /s/	Derived Word: /sh/
critic	**criticize**	**office**	**official**
political	politicize		politician
italics	italicize	artifice	artificial
physics	physicist	prejudice	prejudicial
public	publicize		officiate
cosmetic	cosmetician		
technical	technician		
toxic	toxicity		

Students often confuse the -*ize* and -*yze* endings. There is only a handful of words in American English, however, in which /iz/ is spelled -*yze*, and only two that occur with any degree of frequency: *analyze* and *paralyze*. In contrast, hundreds of words end with the -*ize* spelling.

SORT 18   EXAMINING MULTIPLE ALTERNATIONS

This sort engages students in examining within a set of words the different types of spelling-meaning patterns explored in previous sorts.

Demonstrate

Rather than sorting the words into columns, have students sort words according to spelling-meaning families, putting words that they believe go together in groups. You may need to facilitate this; for example, students may not readily notice that *impunity* goes with *punish* and *punitive*, or *impugn* with *pugnacious* and *pugnacity*. Discuss how these words are related in meaning.

For each spelling-meaning family, have students work singly or in pairs to see how many types of vowel and consonant alternations occur. Look across all of the words, and then group together the words in which there is a long/short vowel alternation (e.g., *defame/defamatory*). Next, group those families in which there is short/schwa alternation (e.g., *triviality/trivial*). Are there families in which more than one type of vowel alternation is occurring? (Yes; for example, *diplomacy/diplomatic*; *diplomacy/diplomatic*.)

For families in which there is a consonant alternation, group together the families in which the sound of the consonant changes, but the spelling stays the same (e.g., *pugnacious/pugnacity*). Next, group families in which the sound and the spelling of the consonants change (e.g., *diver**t**/diver**s**ion/diver**s**e*).

diplomat	defame	trivial	punish
diplomacy	defamatory	triviality	punitive
diplomatic	divert	pugnacious	impunity
syllable	diversion	pugnacity	allege
syllabic	diverse	impugn	allegation
	academy	copy	
	academic	copious	

SORT 19   UNFAMILIAR BUT RELATED WORDS

For most of the word pairs in this sort, students will know one of the words in each pair and therefore be able to determine the meaning of the unfamiliar word. You may wish to scaffold understanding for word pairs such as *perspicacity/perspicacious* and *frugal/frugality*.

Demonstrate

Have students sort words into spelling-meaning families. Two of these families will have three members. Have students discuss possible meanings for unfamiliar words and check their best guesses with one another and the dictionary. Also discuss changes in accent and sound.

Familiar	Unfamiliar	
reciprocate	reciprocity	reciprocal
rhapsody	rhapsodic	
notorious	notoriety	
obsolete	obsolescent	
senator	senatorial	
polar	polarity	
perspicacity	perspicacious	
immune	immunization	immunity
paradigm	paradigmatic	
frugal	frugality	

CUMULATIVE CHECK 3

Ask students to spell and define the following 25 words:

1. condemnation
2. autumnal
3. precision
4. paginate
5. reptilian
6. fragility
7. prohibition
8. centrality
9. mediocre
10. impediment
11. rigidity
12. harmonious
13. proclamation
14. conceive
15. prejudicial
16. artifice
17. defamatory
18. pugnacious
19. impugn
20. defamatory
21. allege
22. reciprocity
23. obsolescent
24. paradigm
25. perspicacious

silent consonant		sounded consonant
sign	**signature**	bomb
soften	resignation	design
columnist	bombard	soft
muscular	designate	muscle
autumn	condemnation	haste
moisten	hasten	resign
column	autumnal	solemn
moist	solemnity	condemn

Words Their Way: Word Sorts for Derivational Relations Spellers © 2006 by Prentice-Hall, Inc.

long vowel		short vowel
type	**typical**	mine
revise	natural	breath
nature	mineral	revision
athletic	nation	gratitude
breathe	grateful	crime
humanity	athlete	national
criminal	humane	ignite
precise	ignition	precision

SORT 11 Vowel Alternation: Long to Short/Schwa

long vowel	short vowel	long vowel	schwa
volcano	**volcanic**		**compose**
composition	reptile		compete
ritual	competition		rite
reptilian	admiration		serene
conspire	conspiracy		admire
custody	serenity		define
page	divine		paginate
definition	custodian		divinity

SORT 12 Adding Suffixes: Vowel Alternation, Accented to Unaccented

base word		derived word
similar	**similarity**	familiar
fragile	invite	combine
invitation	familiarity	fragility
mobile	combination	legal
legality	perspiration	metal
opposition	mobility	oppose
metallic	prohibition	perspire
preside	prohibit	president

SORT 13 Adding Suffix -ity: Vowel Alternation, Schwa to Short

unaccented schwa		accented short
moral	**morality**	mental
general	individuality	generality
individual	mentality	central
brutal	personality	brutality
personal	neutrality	centrality
eventual	originality	eventuality
musical	normality	musicality
original	neutral	normal

Words Their Way: Word Sorts for Derivational Relations Spellers © 2006 by Prentice-Hall, Inc.

base word		derived word
impose	**imposition**	suffice
sufficient	humidity	Iran
humid	Palestinian	mediocre
precocious	Iranian	Palestine
ferocity	Oregonian	impede
Oregon	impediment	Jefferson
specific	Jeffersonian	ferocious
specify	precocity	mediocrity

accent change		no change
comedy	**comedian**	**narrate**
narrative	history	historian
harmony	emphasis	mandatory
emphatic	harmonious	mandate
labor	illustrative	rigid
rigidity	laborious	illustrate
tutorial	janitorial	tutor
majority	major	janitor

Words Their Way: Word Sorts for Derivational Relations Spellers © 2006 by Prentice-Hall, Inc.

base *-m*	*-ation*	base *-e*	*-ption*
exclaim	**exclamation**	**assume**	
assumption	proclamation	acclaim	
acclamation	consumption	presume	
explain	presumption	proclaim	
consume	presumptive	explanation	
conception	reclamation	conceive	
reception	resume	reclaim	
receive	receptive	resumption	

SORT 17 Adding Suffixes: Other Consonant Alternations

base word /k/	derived word /s/	base word /s/	derived word /sh/
critic	**criticize**		**office**
official	political		italics
italicize	artificial		politicize
politician	physicist		artifice
physics	prejudicial		public
cosmetic	publicize		prejudice
technical	cosmetician		toxicity
toxic	technician		officiate

Words Their Way: Word Sorts for Derivational Relations Spellers © 2006 by Prentice-Hall, Inc.

diplomat	defame	trival
punish	diplomacy	diverse
academy	defamatory	diplomatic
syllable	pugnacious	triviality
diversion	copious	divert
academic	punitive	syllabic
impugn	pugnacity	allege
impunity	allegation	copy

Words Their Way: Word Sorts for Derivational Relations Spellers © 2006 by Prentice-Hall, Inc.

SORT 19   Unfamiliar but Related Words

Familiar		Unfamiliar
reciprocate	reciprocity	reciprocal
rhapsody	notorious	senator
polar	rhapsodic	immune
obsolete	obsolescent	notoriety
senatorial	perspicacity	polarity
immunity	immunization	paradigm
frugal	perspicacious	frugality
	paradigmatic	

Words Their Way: Word Sorts for Derivational Relations Spellers © 2006 by Prentice-Hall, Inc.

SORTS 20-28

Greek and Latin Elements I

NOTES FOR THE TEACHER

In sorts 20–28 we begin the more systematic and formal exploration of Greek and Latin elements and their combinations. When students look up the origins of the polysyllabic words they encounter in middle school and high school, they will see that many of those words come from Latin and Greek. The generative nature of English becomes evident in the study of Greek and Latin elements. Often, when we need a new term, especially when we need scientific names, we go back to these elements. Students who are taking biology are likely to encounter hundreds of words such as these, and an understanding of how Latin and Greek elements work will help with the vocabulary load they need to acquire.

When discussing meaningful elements in words that are neither prefixes nor suffixes, linguists make a terminological distinction between elements that come from Latin and elements that come from Greek. The term **word root** is applied to elements that come from Latin; the term **combining form** is applied to elements that come from Greek. It is not necessary to make this distinction with students; the term **root** usually works well enough for both Greek and Latin elements and is also more common.

Throughout this unit you will want students to find other words that share the same elements and to add these to their word study notebooks. It may be easier to brainstorm words than to actually find them in reading materials because the words become far less common as we progress through this unit of study. As mentioned before, words with prefixes are easy to find in dictionaries, but when the element comes later in the word it is a challenge. Searching online dictionaries such as **www.yourdictionary.com** with the use of an asterisk (e.g., *spec**) can turn up additional words; another excellent word and pattern search website is **www.onelook.com**.

We begin with Greek word roots or **combining forms** because they occur fairly frequently in printed materials from the intermediate grades onward *and* their meaning is also relatively concrete and straightforward. Sorts 20 and 21 begin with number and size prefixes and their combination with bases and roots. As part of their study, we will introduce a number of roots to which these prefixes attach and simply mention their meanings; more systematic exploration of Latin roots will begin with sort 24. Because the meanings and nature of Latin roots are often not as straightforward and conceptually transparent as are those of Greek roots, sorts 24 and 25 each involve only two Latin roots; there are also fewer words in these sorts. Beginning with sort 26, the number of Latin roots investigated increases to four.

The selection and sequencing of roots is based on their semantic transparency and the types of elements with which they combine. (See Chapter 8 in *Words Their Way* for further explanation of scope and sequence.) At this phase of word study during the derivational relations stage, students will continue to explore base word/derived word spelling-meaning patterns. This is also the point, however, at which more focused exploration of Greek and Latin word elements can begin—thus the inclusion of these sorts at this point in the scope and sequence of word study.

SORT 20   GREEK AND LATIN NUMBER PREFIXES (*MONO-*, *BI-*, *TRI-*)

This sort introduces the Greek prefix *mono-*, which means "one," and extends an examination of the Latin prefixes of *bi-*, which means "two," and *tri-*, which means "three," to which students are usually introduced earlier. The Latin prefix *uni-* is introduced earlier in a scope and sequence because it occurs with more frequency than does *mono-*.

Background Information

You may mention a number of roots, combining forms, and their meanings in the context of this sort; many of them will be addressed more systematically in later sorts. For example, have students heard the word *triathlon*? *Triathlete*? Do they see a similarity between *triathlon* and *athletic*? Where have they heard *trilogy*? (Most students will probably mention the *Lord of the Rings*; others may mention *Star Wars* or other science fiction trilogies.) What is a *tripod*? Tell students that *pod* is a Greek root that means "foot." In that context, *tripod* makes even more sense; does this now give them a clue to what a *monopod* might be? If someone speaks in a *monotone*, would it be interesting and exciting to listen to them? Similarly, if you speak about the *monotony* of a situation or experience, would that situation or experience be exciting? Since *bi-* means "two" and *sect* comes from *section*, what does it mean to say that an interstate highway *bisects* a city?

As a point of interest, tell students that in English we also have, of course, the word *two*: Have they thought about the relationship between *two*, *twin*, and *twice*? How about *three* and *thrice*?

Demonstrate

Have students sort the words according to the prefixes *mono-*, *bi-*, or *tri-*. Have them discuss the meanings of the words they recognize. In this context, ask them to discuss the difference between *monolingual* and *bilingual*, explicitly referring to what *lingual* means ("language"). This discussion will help establish how these words may be analyzed according to prefix and the remaining meaning element. Students will then have activated their prior knowledge about these prefixes enough to support analyzing the less-familiar words.

mono-	*bi-*	*tri-*
monolingual	**bilingual**	**triangle**
monologue	biennial	tricolor
monopod	bisect	triennial
monopoly	binary	trilogy
monorail	bimonthly	trigonometry
monotone	biweekly	tripod
monotony	bicameral	tricentennial
	biceps	triathlon
		triplets

Extend

What other *bi* and *tri* words can the students think of? Suggest additional ones that they may not mention; for example, *triad, triceratops*. The number "three" is significant in mythology and religion. Have students be on the lookout for significant occurrences of "three."

SORT 21   GREEK AND LATIN ELEMENTS: SIZE (*MICRO-, MEGA-, SUPER-, HYPER-*)

Sort 21 continues the focus on Greek combining forms: *micro-*, which means "small"; *mega-*, which means "great"; *hyper-*, which means "over" or "beyond"; and the inclusion of one Latin form: *super-*, which means "over" or "above." The primary objective is to examine, discuss, and understand how the meanings of these elements combine to result in the meaning of a word. Introduce the sort by telling the students that a large number of words contain these elements, three of which come from Greek and one from Latin. As with the elements examined in sort 20, understanding the meaning of these elements and how they combine will be extremely helpful to the students in learning new vocabulary. We suggest a more explicit walk-through of these words; therefore, the background information is shared in the *Demonstrate* segment of this sort.

Demonstrate

Have the students sort the words by the elements *micro-, mega-, super-,* and *hyper-*. After they have completed the sort, have them discuss the *micro* words. Most students already have an idea, of course, about the meaning of *micro-*, but it is important for them to think explicitly about the way in which it combines. You may say: "*Microscope* is literally aiming or targeting something very small." *Microphone* literally means "small sound," so discuss how a microphone is not *literally* a small sound but that it is a device that picks up sounds that otherwise would not be heard very well. For the word *microcosm*, share the following quote from the Russian developmental psychologist Lev Vygotsky: "A word is a *microcosm* of human experience." Students will realize that this refers to a small part of experience; ask them if they can think of any other words that have *cosm* in them. Share that *cosm* comes from the Greek form *cosmo-*, meaning "order, world/universe." The ancient Greeks conceived of the world or universe as a well-ordered entity. Therefore, the word *cosmos* refers to a well-ordered universe, and *cosmopolitan* refers to something of "worldly" importance. Then, go back to *microcosm*: A word is a "small world" of human experience—not just a "small part"—because each word represents so much of human experience. *Microbe* is a combination of *micro* and *biology*, literally, "small form of life."

The meanings of *super-* and *hyper-* are similar. Most of the words in this sort lend themselves to a straightforward presentation, but students should still analyze each word and reflect on how the prefix and base word combine to result in the meaning of the word.

micro-	*mega-*	*super-*	*hyper-*
microphone	**megaphone**	**supercomputer**	**hypercritical**
microcosm	megalopolis	superhero	hyperactive
microscope	megabyte	superhighway	hyperventilate
Micronesia	megadose	superhuman	hypervigilant
microfilm	megahit	superimpose	hyperirritable
microsurgery			
microbe			
micrometer			

Extend

Contrast *hyper-* with *hypo-*, which means *under, below*, or *beneath*. Students may be familiar with *hypothermia* (lowered temperature) or *hypodermic* (under the skin). Have students generate other words that include *micro-, mega-, super-*, and *hyper-*. Some may be actual words, others may not. For each word generated, they should write a brief definition and/or sentence that includes the word appropriately.

SORT 22   GREEK ROOTS (*AUTO-, BIO-, GEO-, GRAPH-, METER-, PERI-, PHON-, PHOTO-, TELE-*)

This sort offers robust opportunities for exploring these Greek elements and how they work: *auto-*, which means "self"; *bio-*, which means "life"; *geo-*, which means "earth"; *graph-*, which means "write"; *meter-*, which means "measure"; *peri-*, which means "around"; *phon-*, which means "sound"; *photo-*, which means "light"; and *tele-*, which means "distant." When these elements combine with other Greek elements, the resulting meaning is usually obvious or transparent. Students should think directly about the meaning of each of these elements and examine, discuss, and understand how the meanings of these word parts combine to result in the meaning of a word. (Note: There are no headers or example words for this sort because each element is used more than once.) As with the previous sort, we suggest the following more explicit walk-through.

Demonstrate

Introduce this sort by telling the students that many words contain these Greek roots and that these roots usually have a pretty consistent meaning. They usually do not occur by themselves as words, although sometimes they do. Tell the students that learning the meanings of these roots and understanding how they combine to create words will be extremely helpful in figuring out and learning new vocabulary through their reading as well as in correcting occasional spelling errors.

Begin by writing the familiar words *television* and *telephone* on the board or the overhead. Ask students if they see a smaller word within *television* (*vision*). How about *telephone* (*phone*)? Then tell them that *tele* comes from Greek and means "distant." When *tele* combines with *vision*, it literally means "vision from a distance." Discuss why this is, literally, what *television* is and does—it delivers vision from a distance (by cable, satellite, or antenna). Next, discuss that *phone* in *telephone* actually comes from a Greek word that means *sound*. When it combines with *tele*, it literally means "sound from a distance."

Have the students sort all the *-tele-* words. Have them take turns talking about how the meaning of each results from the combination of *-tele-* with another word. Elicit definitions and explanations from the students, though you may need to scaffold their explanations for particular words. For example, *telegraph* contains another word that comes from Greek, *graph*, which means "writing." Students have probably heard about the *telegraph*, but perhaps not thought about the fact that it means, literally, "writing from a distance." You may need to scaffold discussion of *telephoto*; the students have probably heard the word in the context of a telephoto lens but not reflected on the meaning. Tell them that *photo* also comes from Greek and means "light." This often leads to a productive discussion about the literal meaning of *telephoto*—"light from a distance." As for *telescope*, tell them that *scope* is also a word that originally came from Greek and means "target" or "aim"; what, then, does *telescope* literally mean? Similarly, *periscope* literally means to "aim" or "target" around.

Next, sort the *graph* words. Discuss *photography*—literally "writing with light"—because there is usually at least one student who understands the process by which photography works. If not, this may be a good time to mention the process briefly; for example, the lens lets in light that is "written" onto film or a disk (as with a digital camera).

Continue with other roots. Have students discuss the unfamiliar terms, debating what the meaning might be, based on their inference from the combination of the word parts. Discussion of how the meanings of the Greek forms combine to result in the meaning of each word is critical.

This is also a good time to mention how the prefix *sym-/syn-* works. Meaning "together, with," *sym-/syn-* occurs with considerable frequency, and also comes from Greek. Tell students that *synthesis* means combining or bringing together separate pieces to form a whole. The word *photosynthesis*, therefore, literally means "bringing together" or "synthesizing" light. Share with the students that they don't have to go into the details of photosynthesis, which probably are understandable only to biologists anyway. They need only to understand that photosynthesis is an important process that plants utilize to stay alive and grow.

A good practice is to xerox a table of Greek word roots and place it in the students' vocabulary notebooks for ready reference (see Table 8-6 in Chapter 8 of *Words Their Way*).

photograph	periscope	autobiography	symphony
photosynthesis	geothermal	biography	phonology
television	geology	biorhythms	phonograph
telecommunication	biology	autograph	phonics
telegraph	perimeter	automobile	telephone
telescope	thermometer		
telephoto	barometer		
	micrometer		

Extend

How many words have multiple meanings? For example, *telegraph* can also have the sense of *telegraphing* one's intent to another. So, though we don't use the original meaning of *telegraph* that often anymore, we *do* use the more metaphorical or *connotative* meaning. This may be a good opportunity to discuss the concept of *connotation*, which has to do with the meaning that is *suggested* by the word and *associations* that may be made with the word.

On an etymological note, after discussing what *bioscope* might mean, you can share with the students that *bioscope* was the name for an early movie projector. How do they think this word came about?

A spelling convention began in Roman times in which a "connecting vowel" was often inserted between two word parts: If one word part ends with a consonant and the next word part begins with a consonant, a vowel—usually *o* or *i*—is inserted; for example, *thermometer*, *phonograph*.

Activity 8-10 in *Words Their Way*, "Combining Roots and Affixes," is an excellent follow-up activity to this sort, as well as to later sorts in which Greek and Latin elements are explored.

SORT 23   NUMBER PREFIXES (*QUADR-, TETRA-, QUINT-, PENT-, DEC-*)

This sort discusses number prefixes: *quadr-* and *tetra-*, which both mean "four"; *quint-* and *pent-*, which both mean "five"; and *dec-*, which means "ten."

Demonstrate

Have students sort the words according to number prefix. Have them discuss any words they know or at least have seen or heard. Speculate as to their meaning. If *triad* refers to a group of three, for example, what does a *tetrad* refer to? If *tripod* refers to three feet, what does *tetrapod* refer to? Share the following sentence with students: "Scientists reported to-day that they discovered the leg bone of the oldest known amphibian, a *tetrapod* that lived 360 million years ago." If *monarchy* refers to rule by a single person—a king or a queen—then what might a *tetrarchy* refer to? A *pentarchy*? While students may know that *quintuplets* refers to five siblings born at the same time, share with them that the word *quintessence*, which refers to the purest or highest essence of something—"She was the *quintessence* of gymnastic ability"—historically and literally means the fifth and highest "essence" after the essences of air, earth, fire, and water. The sentence "We now have the *quintessential* recipe for tacos" means that the recipe is the most representative one for tacos.

Discuss why there seem to be so many words and elements derived from Greek that refer to *athletics*. This may evolve into an exploration of the value the Greeks placed on physical prowess and beauty.

Now that several number prefixes have been explored, share with the students *why* there are different prefixes for "one," "two," "four," "five," and so forth: Greek had its own words for these elements, Latin had other words. Both sets of number elements survived and continued to be passed down through other languages without significant change.

quadr-	tetra-	quint-	pent-	dec-
quadruple	tetrad	**quintuple**	**pentagon**	**decimal**
quadruplets	tetrarchy	quintuplets	pentangle	decathlon
quadrangle	tetralogy	quintessence	pentathlon	decathlete
quadruped	tetrapod	quintessential	pentathlete	decimate
quadrennial			pentarchy	
quadrant			pentad	

Extend

Have students collect other words they come across that contain number prefixes and write them in their vocabulary notebooks. If the meaning of a word is not obvious, they should write the sentence in which it occurs as well.

SORT 24   LATIN WORD ROOTS (-*SPECT*-, -*PORT*-)

This sort discusses the Latin roots -*spect*-, which means "to look at"; and -*port*-, which means "to carry." The meanings of these Latin roots are straightforward, as are the meanings of most of the words in which they combine with other affixes and roots. As with the Greek roots or combining forms in sort 22, these Latin roots occur frequently in printed materials from the intermediate grades onwards.

Demonstrate

Because this sort is the first of many that will explore Latin word roots, you may wish to begin by walking the students through two or three words, explaining how the elements combine to produce the meaning of the word. (The teacher scripts in Chapter 8 of *Words Their Way* are good models for this type of explanation.) There are fewer words in this sort, in order to focus attention on the concept of a *root* as a meaningful element.

Begin by writing the words *inspection* and *export* on the board or the overhead. Ask the students to explain the meaning of *inspection*, and use the word in a sentence. Then tell them that the word is made up of the suffix -*ion* (the "act or result" of something), the Latin root -*spec*-, which means "to look at," and the prefix -*in*, meaning "into." Now have the students think about it: Given their explanation and definition of *inspection*, do they see that the combination of these word parts literally means "the act of looking into" something? Repeat this process with *export:* Have the students discuss what the word means, then show them that the word comes from the Latin root *-port-,* which means "to carry," and the prefix *ex-,* meaning "out." Now have the students think about it: Given their explanation and definition of *export,* do they see that the combination of the root *-port-* with the prefix *ex-* literally means "carrying out"? (You may mention *import* as well here: Tell them the prefix *im-* means "in, into." Is it clear how *export* and *import* are related?)

After the introduction, have students sort the words according to the root in each. Follow up by having students discuss, in pairs, how they think the word parts combine to produce the meaning of each word. *Circumspect* is the one word in this sort whose precise meaning is more connotative than literal; putting the word parts together yields the meaning "to look around." Discuss the *connotative* meaning of the word—the meaning that is *suggested* by the word and the *associations* that may be made with the word: When you behave in a *circumspect* manner, you look around and are careful because you are thinking of the possible results of what you are doing.

Following are other words that you may walk through with the students after they sort and discuss them: *perspective,* "look through" (when you talk about your *perspective* on an issue or on life you are actually talking about how you have *looked through* that issue); *prospect,* "look forward." Point out to the students that, for the vast majority of words that appear to contain a word root, they can best analyze the words by beginning at the end of the word: Reflect on how you analyzed the words *inspect, circumspect,* and *export.*

-spect-	*-port-*
inspection	**export**
perspective	deport
retrospect	import
spectator	transport
circumspect	report
prospect	portfolio
introspect	heliport
spectacle	portage
spectacular	importune
spectrum	opportune
	supportable

Extend

Several words offer possibilities for generating additional words derived from them by adding *-ion* or *-ation.* Have students see how many derived words they can generate, first by discussing whether the derived words really exist or not, and then checking the dictionary to confirm or not; for example, *retrospection* or *retrospectation? importation* or *importion?*

SORT 25   LATIN WORD ROOTS (-*DIC-*, -*AUD-*)

This sort discusses the Latin roots *-dic-,* which means "to say or speak"; and *-aud-,* which means "to hear." As with sort 24, the meanings of these Latin roots are straightforward, as are the meanings of most of the words in which they combine with other affixes and roots. As with the previous sort, fewer words are examined in order to highlight and focus on the concept of a *root.*

Demonstrate

Begin by writing the words *dictate* and *audible* on the board or the overhead. Ask the students to explain the meaning of *dictate* and use the word in a sentence. Continue this introduction with the word *audible*. Depending on the students' response, encourage them to speculate about the meanings of the roots *-dic-* and *-aud-*. Sort the words and discuss the meanings of other words to help the students arrive at some conclusions about the meanings of the roots. *Laudable* is an "oddball"; it means "praiseworthy" and does not contain the root *aud*.

Following are other words that you may walk through with the students after they sort and discuss them: *verdict* actually has two roots, *-ver-* meaning "truth" and *-dic-*, "to say or speak"; *unpredictable*—after *un-* and *-able* are removed, the base word *predict* remains. Literally, *predict* means "to say before"; put *-able* back on and discuss what *predictable* means, then put *un-* back on and discuss what *unpredictable* means. *Benediction* contains not only the root *-dic-*, but the root *-bene-* as well, meaning "good." So, *benediction* literally means "good saying" and usually refers to the blessing at the end of many religious services.

-dic-	-aud-	
dictate	**audible**	laudable
contradict	auditorium	
unpredictable	auditory	
verdict	audience	
diction	audiology	
edict	audiotape	
dictionary	inaudible	
dictator	audition	
benediction		
indict		

SORT 26   LATIN WORD ROOTS (-*GRESS*-, -*RUPT*-, -*TRACT*-, -*MOT*-)

This sort discusses the Latin roots *-gress-*, which means "to go"; *-rupt-*, which means "to break"; *-tract-*, which means "to draw or pull"; and *-mot-*, which means "to move." As with the roots in the previous two sorts, these roots occur with considerable frequency.

Background Information

Progress = *gress* "to go" + *pro* "forward"—so *progress* literally means "to move forward."

Interrupt = *rupt* "to break" + *inter* "between"—so *interrupt* literally means "to break in between," which is what you do when you *interrupt* a conversation.

Detract = *tract* "to draw or pull" + *de* "away, apart"—so *detract* literally means "to draw away from," which is what happens when something *detracts* from what you want people to pay attention to. ("Your hollering about why you like your candidate *detracts* from your goal of getting people to vote for her.")

Promote = *mot(e)* "to move" + *pro* "forward"—so when you *promote* an idea, you move that idea forward.

Demonstrate

Have the students sort the words according to the root. As in the previous sort, have students pair up to discuss the meanings of each of the words. Then regroup to discuss any of the words about which they were uncertain; in this context you will simply mention the appropriate elements and their meanings. Tell the students that they may notice these elements in other words, but that you will be exploring the elements in depth later on. For example, *attract* and *aggression* actually contain the absorbed prefix *ad-*, meaning "to or toward"; this and other absorbed prefixes are addressed in sorts 49 and 50. In several of the words *e-* is a prefix meaning "out"; for example, when a volcano *erupts* it literally "breaks out"; *emotion* literally means "the act or result of moving out"—discuss with students how this word has come to possess the connotative meaning it has now. When someone is *emotional*, what "moves out" from within them? Point out that the base word of *emotion* is *emote*, a word that we don't run across nearly as often as *emotion*. Where do they think the word *emoticon* comes from? What word is combined with *emotion/emote* to create *emoticon*? (*icon*)

-gress-	-rupt-	-tract-	-mot-
progress	**interrupt**	**detract**	**promote**
regress	erupt	distract	promotion
digress	rupture	traction	demote
aggression	abrupt	attract	demotion
egress	disrupt	protract	emote
transgress		tractor	emotion
			emoticon

SORT 27 LATIN WORD ROOTS (-*FRACT*-, -*FLECT*-/ -*FLEX*-, -*JECT*-, -*MIS*-/-*MIT*-)

This sort discusses the Latin roots -*fract*-, meaning "to break"; -*flect*-/-*flex*-, meaning "to bend"; -*ject*-, meaning "to throw"; and -*mis*-/-*mit*-, meaning "to send."

Demonstrate

Have the students sort the words according to root. Have them sort individually, and then have them compare their sorts with those of a partner to see if they had different categories. Some students will sort according to the spelling of the root so that words containing -*flex*- and -*flect*-, for example, will be in different groups. Have the students then discuss what they think each root means. Guide their discussion by focusing first on the more obvious or literally apparent combinations: for example, *fraction* is "the result of breaking" something into smaller pieces; *reject* is to "throw back." You may facilitate discussion of some of the more semantically opaque combinations, such as *objection*. An *objection* is, literally, "the act or result of throwing against" (*ob* means "against"). More connotatively, making an *objection* is "throwing" a verbal point against someone. Mention *permission*: Which word does it come from? How about *transmission*? Mention also that *trajectory* actually comes from the combination of the prefix *trans-* "across" + -*ject*-, literally "to throw across"; "the long *trajectory* of the soccer ball as it soared over the heads of the other team." *Fractious* actually comes from an old sense of *fraction*, which meant "discord." If you use the word *fractious* to refer to someone's behavior, how might you characterize or describe that behavior?

-fract-	-flect-/-flex-	-ject-	-mis-/-mit-
fracture	**reflect**	**reject**	**transmit**
fraction	flexible	project	emit
infraction	deflect	projectile	remit
fractious	reflex	injection	permit
refract		eject	omit
		trajectory	mission
		objection	submit
			submission

Extend

What other words can the students create with other affixes (e.g., *inflexible* or *flexiblity*)? Review the suffix and spelling changes when the suffix is added in *projection, rejection, deflection, reflection, emission, omission,* and so forth.

SORT 28   LATIN WORD ROOTS (-*MAN*-, -*SCRIB*-/ -*SCRIPT*-, -*CRED*-, -*FAC*-)

This sort discusses the Latin roots -*man*-, meaning "hand"; -*scrib*-/-*script*-, meaning "to write"; -*cred*-, meaning "to believe"; and -*fac*-, meaning "to make."

Background Information

Man and *scrib/script* are usually straightforward—*manual* labor is working by hand, *manuscript* is writing by hand. Students will probably be quite curious about *manure,* however! Share with them that, etymologically, *manure* is actually closely related to *manual: Manure* evolved from a Middle English word that meant "to cultivate land," which in turn evolved from a Latin word that meant "to work with the hands." Ask the students how they think people hundreds of years ago actually cultivated their land, knowing what they know about the present-day meaning of *manure.*

Contrast *credible* and *incredible. Incredible* is the more common word. Discuss its meaning, then ask students what they think *credible* means. Scaffold their understanding that if something is *incredible,* it is literally "not believable." *Credence* may also be unfamiliar: "Because she is so knowledgeable about setting up a website, I put a lot of *credence* in her advice."

The way the root -*fac*- works in *factory* and *manufacture* is straightforward. Ask students if they see a familiar pattern in *facsimile.* After *fac* is removed, *simile* remains. What do they think *simile* might mean? For most students, this is the first time they become aware that "similar" is in *facsimile*—literally, "make similar." Isn't that what a *fax* machine does? (This may also be the first time that students realize *fax* is short for *facsimile.*) *Artifact* is a good example of a word whose literal sum of its meaning parts—"something made from art"—no longer exactly fits, but allows you to discuss a more connotative meaning: Something made by humans at a different time and in a different culture.

Ascribe—literally, "to write to"—can be introduced with the sentence "I *ascribe* Devon's sleeping in class to his staying up late every night watching DVDs." After discussing some of the *scrib/script* words, ask students where the word *scribble* came from—most students will not have consciously made this connection.

Demonstrate

On the first day, work with the words as you did in sort 23. Students may sort these words without teacher introduction. Have them first sort individually, then compare with a partner. Students will notice that *manufacture* and *manuscript* may be sorted in more than one category. Ask them to discuss with their partners what they think each root might mean. After partner discussions, discuss the meanings that the students have generated. Address roots about which the students are uncertain.

On the second day of working with these words, you may elect to discuss why the spelling of some roots changes across related words (e.g., *scrib/script; fac/fic/fect*). These forms come from the original Latin verbs, in which the sound changed in different forms, and therefore the spelling changed as well. This is similar to what happens in many English verbs: We *come* to visit today/we *came* to visit yesterday; I will *run* quickly/I *ran* quickly.

-man-	-scrib-/-script-	-cred-	-fac-
manual	**circumscribe**	**incredible**	**factory**
manuscript	prescribe	credible	manufacture
manicure	prescription	credence	facsimile
manure	inscribe	discredit	facilitate
mandate	inscription	incredulous	artifact
maneuver	transcribe		
	postscript		
	ascribe		

Extend

Ask students to generate other *scrib/script* words ending in *-ion* (e.g., *subscribe/subscription; transcribe/transcription*).

By this point, students have explored a sufficient number of Latin and Greek elements to play *Greek and Latin Jeopardy* (see Chapter 8 of *WTW*). This is an extremely popular game format with students and is one that will continue to grow with the students' advancing word knowledge. Eventually students can prepare their own *Jeopardy* games, exploring new roots as well as using the format to develop and reinforce content-area vocabulary in science, math, and social studies, for example. Other Greek- and Latin-element games in Chapter 8 of *WTW* may also be explored here and in subsequent units.

CUMULATIVE CHECK 4

Ask students to spell and define the following words:

1. monotony
2. tricentennial
3. microsurgery
4. hypercritical
5. telecommunication
6. geothermal
7. quadruped
8. quintessence
9. retrospect
10. opportune
11. edict
12. inaudible
13. contradict
14. aggression
15. interrupt
16. protract
17. trajectory
18. incredulous
19. facsimile
20. circumscribe

mono-	bi-	tri-
monolingual	**bilingual**	**triangle**
biceps	monologue	biennial
monopod	tripod	tricolor
bisect	triennial	monopoly
trilogy	monorail	binary
monotone	trigonometry	bicameral
biweekly	tricentennial	monotony
triathlon	bimonthly	triplets

SORT 21 Greek and Latin Elements: Size (*micro-*, *mega-*, *super-*, *hyper-*)

micro-	*mega-*	*super-*	*hyper-*
microphone	**megaphone**	**supercomputer**	
megabyte	**hypercritical**	microsurgery	
microcosm	superhero	hyperventilate	
megadose	hyperactive	superhighway	
megahit	microscope	megalopolis	
micrometer	superhuman	hypervigilant	
microfilm	Micronesia	superimpose	
microbe		hyperirritable	

SORT 22   Greek Roots (-*auto*-, -*bio*-, -*geo*-, -*graph*-, -*meter*-, -*peri*-, -*phon*-, -*photo*-, -*tele*-)

telecommunication		photosynthesis
photograph	autobiography	periscope
symphony	biorhythms	television
geothermal	phonograph	biography
phonology	thermometer	telegraph
telescope	perimeter	phonics
biology	telephone	geology
telephoto	barometer	micrometer
autograph	automobile	

quadr-	tetra-	quint-	pent-	dec-

quadruple	tetrad	quintuple
pentagon	decimal	quadruplets
tetrarchy	quintuplets	pentangle
decathlon	quadrangle	tetralogy
quintessence	pentathlon	decathlete
quadruped	tetrapod	pentathlete
quintessential	decimate	pentarchy
quadrennial	quadrant	pentad

-spect-	*-port-*	
inspection	**export**	perspective
deport	retrospect	spectator
import	transport	report
prospect	circumspect	introspect
spectacle	portfolio	heliport
portage	spectacular	importune
spectrum	opportune	supportable

SORT 25   Latin Roots (*-dic-*, *-aud-*)

-dic-	*-aud-*	
dictate	**audible**	contradict
verdict	unpredictable	diction
laudable	auditorium	edict
dictator	dictionary	auditory
audience	audiology	audiotape
benediction	inaudible	audition
indict		

-gress-	*-rupt-*	*-tract-*	*-mot-*
progress	**interrupt**		**detract**
promote	regress		erupt
distract	promotion		digress
rupture	traction		demote
aggression	abrupt		attract
demotion	egress		disrupt
protract	emote		transgress
tractor	emotion		emoticon

Words Their Way: Word Sorts for Derivational Relations Spellers © 2006 by Prentice-Hall, Inc.

SORT 27   Latin Roots (-fract-, -flect-/-flex-, -ject-, -mis-/-mit-)

-fract-	-flect-/-flex-	-ject-	-mis-/-mit-
fracture	**reflect**		**reject**
transmit	fraction		flexible
project	emit		infraction
deflect	projectile		remit
fractious	reflex		injection
permit	refract		eject
omit	trajectory		mission
submit	objection		submission

SORT 28   Latin Roots (*-man-*, *-scrib-/-script-*, *-cred-*, *-fac-*)

-man-	*-scrib-/-script-*	*-cred-*	*-fac-*
manual	**circumscribe**		**incredible**
factory	manuscript		prescribe
credible	manufacture		manicure
facsimile	prescription		credence
manure	inscription		mandate
facilitate	incredulous		artifact
transcribe	postscript		ascribe
discredit	maneuver		inscribe

SORTS 29–34

Greek and Latin Elements II

NOTES FOR THE TEACHER

In addition to some common, straightforward elements, many of the elements explored in this section are elements that have evolved from their literal meaning to a more connotative meaning. They are studied because they occur across a wide range of content areas and domains. In addition, several of the roots are grouped topically, such as those related to *government* and the *body*.

SORT 29 LATIN WORD ROOTS (-*JUD*-, -*LEG*-, -*MOD*-, -*BIBLIO*-)

Sort 29 discusses the Latin roots *-jud-,* meaning "to judge"; *-leg-,* meaning "law" or "to read"; *-mod-,* meaning "model," "moderate," or "mode"; and *-biblio-,* meaning "book."

Background Information

Because of the nature of these roots and their combinations, a substantial amount of background information is included in the *Demonstrate* section as part of a more explicit explanation.

Demonstrate

Have the students sort the words according to roots without teacher introduction, discuss them with a partner, and afterwards share any uncertainties they have about how particular words should be categorized. For example, the *-leg-* root may not be obvious in *privilege* and *allegiance.*

Ask the students what they think the root *-jud-* means, and if they are uncertain, write the word *judge* on the board. Then, discuss how *prejudice* literally means "judge before"—people who are *prejudiced* have already judged another person or idea, for example. When a judge *adjudicates* a case she "hears and settles" the case; literally, the word *adjudicate* means "to judge to or toward" something (*ad-* is a prefix meaning "to or toward").

Next, discuss the *biblio* words. Students may have a good idea about the meaning of this root. Begin with *bibliography,* a written list of books. Students may note that *biblical* is related to *Bible*—perhaps the first time they may have thought about the word *Bible* meaning "book." (*Bibliophile* offers an opportunity to mention the Greek combining form *phile,* which means "having a strong preference for, loving." Some examples include

Philadelphia, "city of love," and *anglophile,* someone who loves England and things English.) *Bibliotheca* is "a collection of books." Students who are studying Spanish or whose first language is Spanish will notice the relationship of this word to the word for "library" in Spanish—*biblioteca.*

Have the students work in pairs to sort words that have the *-leg-* root into two categories: words that have to do with *law* and words that have to do with *reading* or literacy. This process will not be entirely straightforward, so after they have sorted and discussed the words, bring the students back together and do a group sort. Discuss words about which they are uncertain, and if necessary share with them the following information: *Legend, legible,* and *legion* all come from an Indo-European root that means "to gather or collect." If something is *legible,* one can *read* it, "gathering or collecting" information; *legend* comes from a Latin word meaning something that was "to be read," referring to written stories. The word *legion* more directly refers to a "gathering" of individuals, as in its original meaning in Roman times: In the military, the Roman *legion* was the basic unit of organization in the army. *Privilege* actually contains two roots—*-priv-* ("single, alone" as in *private*) and *-leg-*—and it means, literally, "law for an individual."

Moderate relates to "measure" in that it refers to keeping within reasonable limits, as when one is a *moderate* eater or eats *moderately.* You may wish to tell the students that *accommodate* is one of the words most frequently misspelled by highly literate adults: They usually leave out one *m.* Walking through its etymology *may* help this confusion; at the very least, it will provide students with more information to associate with the spelling. *Accommodate* is related to *commodious* (literally, "to measure with"), which means "spacious, roomy", and so *accommodate* has come to mean "to make room for." When you *accommodate* someone you "make room for" them or for their wishes, ideas, or point of view. The most common meaning for *mode* is the "manner" of doing something, which in fact is a meaning that goes back to the Latin word for *mode*—"manner" or "style." If you prefer a particular manner or style of learning something, for example, this is often referred to as a preference for a particular *modality.* Interestingly, this meaning applies to *modern* as well: "in a certain manner, just now."

-jud-	*-leg-*	*-leg-*	*-biblio-*	*-mod-*
prejudice	**legalistic**	**legible**	**bibliography**	**moderate**
adjudicate	legislate	legend	bibliophile	mode
judiciary	allegiance	legion	biblically	modern
	privilege		bibliomania	modernity
			bibliotheca	modality
				accommodate

Extend

The "Greek and Latin Jeopardy" and "Double Latin Root Jeopardy" games in Chapter 8 of *Words Their Way* will be very appropriate for this sort and subsequent root-focused sorts. Students can apply this format to creating their own Jeopardy games incorporating words from other content areas.

SORT 30   LATIN WORD ROOTS (-*BENE-*, -*MAL-*) AND PREFIXES (*ANTE-, POST-*)

This sort discusses the Latin roots *-bene-,* meaning "good or well"; *-mal-,* meaning "bad"; and prefixes *ante-,* meaning "before"; and *post-,* meaning "after."

Background Information

Malfeasance is closely related to *malefactor*. Someone who is accused of *malfeasance* is a person, usually a public official, who "does bad," or more specifically, engages in inappropriate conduct or wrongdoing.

Dismal = "bad day." *Dis* is not a prefix, but rather comes from the Latin *dies*, which means "day." So, *dismal* literally means "bad day."

Malaria = "bad air." Originally the cause of malaria was literally thought to be "bad air." *malice/malicious* comes from the Latin word *malus*, which means "bad."

Maladroit = "not adroit." Ask the students what the base word of *maladroit* is—have they heard of it? If someone is *adroit* at something, what does that mean? So, if someone is **mal**adroit, what does that mean?

Demonstrate

Sort 30 contrasts two word roots, *-bene-* and *-mal-*, and two prefixes, *ante-* and *post-*. The emphasis here is on their combination with other roots and base words, and for the first time, some common Latin phrases are included.

You should introduce only the roots *-bene-* and *-mal-* the first day and point out the ways in which they function within the words. Have the students first sort the words by their root, *-bene-* or *-mal-*. A handful of words may be sorted into different categories. Begin your discussion by asking the students which words they think they know the meaning of, and discuss these. Be sure to elicit from the students the realization that *benefit* has to do with "good." Discuss *malfunction*—if something *malfunctions* does it function well or poorly? Then discuss *benefactor*: Do the students recognize another root they've recently explored (*-fac-* in sort 28, "to make")? A *benefactor*, then, is literally someone who "makes good," or is *beneficial* and *benevolent*—which literally means "good will" (*vol* = "will"). Contrast *benefactor* with *malefactor*.

On the second day, introduce the prefixes *ante-* and *post-* with the words *antedate* and *postdate*. Discuss what *postdate* means, as in *postdate* a check. Then explain that *antedate* literally means "to date before," or more specifically, refers to something that has occurred earlier in time or history: "Bebop *antedates* hip-hop by almost half a century."

Tell the students that they are likely to run into several *ante* and *post* words and phrases in their reading materials. *Antebellum* and *postbellum* literally mean "before the war" and "after the war." In America, *antebellum* most often refers to the time period before the Civil War, as in *antebellum* architecture or *antebellum* attitudes and beliefs. Students have probably heard the term *postmortem*; discuss this and then ask them what *antemortem* probably means. They may also have heard of *ante meridiem* and *post meridiem*—if not, ask them what they think "AM" and "PM" refer to. Share that *meridiem* is a Latin word meaning "midday." *Anterior* and *posterior* refer to "before, in front" and "behind, in back," respectively. (Students may be familiar with the euphemistic use of *posterior* to refer to one's rear end!)

-bene-	*-mal-*	*ante-*	*post-*
benefit	**malfunction**	**antebellum**	**postdate**
beneficial	malevolent	ante meridiem	post meridiem
benefactor	dismal	antedate	postbellum
benevolent	malaria	antemortem	postmortem
	malcontent	anterior	posterior
	malefactor		
	malice		
	malicious		
	maladroit		
	malfeasance		

Extend

Remind students of the name of one of Harry Potter's classmates, Malfoy. J. K. Rowling has created many of the characters' names using Greek and Latin elements. Challenge students to brainstorm other names from the series that give a clue to the personality of the character.

SORT 31   GREEK AND LATIN ELEMENTS: GOVERNMENT (-*CRAT*/-*CRACY*, -*ARCHY*/-*ARCH*-)

This sort examines a number of word roots and combining forms that work with the Greek word parts -*crat*/-*cracy*, meaning "rule or government"; and -*arch*-/-*archy*, meaning "rule." Related words may be paired and discussed.

Background Information

Plutocrat/plutocracy—government or rule by the wealthy or rich.
Aristocrat/aristocracy—literally, rule by "the best," though this has come to mean rule by the nobility and the rich.
Bureaucrat/bureaucracy—literally, rule from "an office."
Theocrat/theocracy—literally, rule by "God," though in fact it is humans who are ruling, but claiming to do so in the name of a god, following his or her precepts.
Oligarch/oligarchy—rule by "a few."
Anarchy/anarchist—in these words, *an-* is a prefix meaning "without" (as in *amoral*). Literally, *anarchy* is "without rule"—there is no government in control.

Demonstrate

Have students work in pairs to match up the base and derived forms, then discuss their possible meanings. Students will have at least heard most of these words, though they may be uncertain about the meanings. Students may check these words in their dictionaries.

-cracy	-crat	-archy	-arch-
autocracy	**autocrat**	**monarchy**	**monarch**
democracy	democrat	oligarchy	oligarch
plutocracy	plutocrat	anarchy	anarchist
aristocracy	aristocrat	hierarchy	hierarchical
bureaucracy	bureaucrat	matriarchy	matriarch
technocracy	technocrat	patriarchy	patriarch

Extend

This is a good point to introduce and continue to use the "It's All Greek to Us" game in Chapter 8 of *Words Their Way*.

SORT 32   GREEK AND LATIN ELEMENTS: AMOUNT (*MAGNI*-, *MACRO*-, *POLY*-, *EQU*-, *OMNI*-)

This sort examines the meanings of the elements *magni-*, which means "great"; *macro-*, which means "large"; *poly-*, which means "much" or "many"; *equ-*, which means "equal"; and *omni-*, which means "all."

Although the meanings of these Greek elements are fairly straightforward, their combination with other elements to form the words in this sort may be a bit opaque. If you wish, you may walk the students through this sort, sharing as much of the following background information as you believe may be helpful.

Background Information

The Greek combining forms usually occur as prefixes and in a very large number of words. So, too, do the Latin prefixes *equ-* and *omni-*. For example, *magnificent* includes the Latin root *-fic-*, which is actually another form of the Latin root *-fac-*, ("make") that was explored in sort 28. So, *magnificent* literally means "to make great."

You may wish to ask students if *macroscopic* reminds them of another word they know. Usually they will suggest *microscope* or *microscopic*—so, what do they think *macroscopic* means? Begin the discussion on the prefix *poly-* with the word *polysyllabic,* which refers to a word that has three or more syllables. Students will probably be familiar with *polygon* (*gon* meaning "angle"); the other *poly* words are probably less familiar to them. *Polymath* is interesting because *math* is a Greek combining form that means "to learn," so the word literally means "to learn much" and usually refers to a person. *Polyglot* also refers to a person—one who knows many languages (*glot* comes from a Greek word meaning "tongue, language"). The other element besides *poly* in *polysemous* is *sem*, which comes from a Greek word meaning "to signify, a sign." A related word is *semantics*, which refers to "meaning," usually in the context of language. So, a *polysemous* word is one that has many meanings—for example, *dog* and *table.*

Equ- is fairly straightforward. Begin your discussion with *equator*, discuss its meanings, and then discuss *equatorial*, which means having to do with or characterizing the equator. An *equation* has to do with things being equal. Discuss what an *equitable* solution refers to. *Equanimity* may be a new term, meaning, literally, "even (equal)-tempered"; so, if someone possesses *equanimity*, they are calm and even-tempered. The end of this word, *animity*, comes from the Latin *animus*, meaning "mind," which in turn is related to Latin *anima* ("life, soul"). This root also occurs in *animal* and *animated* ("living"). Students will probably know the meaning of *equivalent*, but point out that it is made up of *equ-* + *valent*, which comes from the Latin root for "force"—literally, "equal force."

In introducing *omnivore*, ask students to define the word *voracious*. The sense of rabid eating will usually emerge. Then, ask them what an *omnivore* might be. Next, write *science* on the board and ask the students if it gives any clue to *omniscient*. Then tell them that *science* comes from a Latin word meaning "to know." So, *omniscient* means "all knowing." You may wish to introduce the word *prescient* (pronounced "PRESHunt"), as in "She was uncannily *prescient* in her observations about how the election results would turn out." Someone who is *prescient* displays the quality of *prescience* (pronounced "PRESHuns").

Demonstrate

Have the students sort the words by prefixes, discussing the meaning of the words they know and working to infer the meaning of the remainder. They may check their hypotheses in their dictionaries.

magni-	*macro-*	*poly-*	*equ-*	*omni-*
magnificent	**macroscopic**	**polysyllabic**	**equator**	**omnipotent**
magnification	macroeconomics	polygon	equitable	omnivore
magnitude		polymath	equation	omniscient
		polysemous	equanimity	omnidirectional
		polytechnic	equatorial	
		polyglot	equilateral	
			equivalent	

SORT 33   GREEK AND LATIN ELEMENTS: RELATED TO THE BODY (-*CAP*-, -*PED*-/-*POD*-, -*PED*-, -*CORP*-)

Because of the two fundamentally different meanings for each of the roots -*cap*-, which can mean either "head" or "to take," and -*ped*-, which can mean either "foot" or "child," it is best to introduce this sort over two days. In addition, there is -*corp*-, which means "body," and -*pod*-, which also means "foot." In contrast to the previous sort, we suggest that you walk through this sort with your students, providing background information along the way. The sort is set up to provide a back-and-forth dynamic between the information you are providing and the thinking and inferencing in which your students will be engaged.

Demonstrate

On the first day, address -*cap*- and -*ped*-/-*pod*- (foot). Have students sort the words according to word root; they will probably put -*pod*- in a separate column, which is fine. Ask students what *decapitate* means. Their mentioning of "head" allows you to discuss *capital* and *capitol*—these words have to do with "head" of government. But why the difference in spelling? *Capital* refers to the city where the government is located, *capitol* refers to the actual building in which the legislative body of the government meets. *Recapitulate* refers to stating again (*re-*) the main point, the *heading*.

In the word *captivity*, the root -*cap*- comes from a Latin word meaning "to seize." Encourage students to generate other words in which the root has this meaning, for example *captive, captivate.*

-*ped*- and -*pod*- both refer to "foot" (remind students of *monopod, tripod,* and *quadruped*). You may need to tell students what the root means. Most of the -*ped*- words are understandable based on a structural analysis, but discuss them with students to be certain. *Pedicure* has two roots; *cure* means "care of." *Expedite* means to speed up, or execute more quickly. In Latin the root literally meant to free from entanglements, and going back further to Indo-European, "to free one's foot from a snare." *Expedition* is derived from *expedite*. Similarly, *impede* has evolved to mean "obstruct the progress of" something. *Podiatry* means, literally, "the healing of" (-*iatry*) the foot; a *podiatrist* practices *podiatry*. -*iatry* occurs in a number of words, and always refers to healing. The meaning of *podium*, "base," evolved from "foot."

On the second day, address the root -*corp*- by first discussing *corpse*, quite literally a body. Move then to *corps*, which is a military unit or body, or a group such as a press corps. Then discuss how *corporal* and *corporation* reflect the concept of "body." The primary meaning of *corporal* is "having to do with the body"; another meaning, of course, is the designation of a particular rank in the military.

The other meaning of -*ped*-, "child," comes from Greek. *Pedagogy* comes from *pedagogue*, which literally means "one who leads children"; this meaning derives from classical Greece, when a slave took children to and from school. It is a short step from one who leads children to and from school to one who teaches children. *Pediatric* refers to medical practice specializing in the treatment of children. A *pedant* makes a conscious effort to display or show off his learning, so pedantic behavior is characterized by that type of showing off. Interestingly, -*ped*- comes through Latin and means "to instruct," which in turn came from the Greek root, which means "child."

-cap-	-ped-/-pod-	-ped-	-corp-
decapitate	**pedestrian**	**pediatric**	**corpse**
capitol	pedicure	pediatrician	corps
capital	pedestal	pedagogy	corpulent
captivity	centipede	pedagogue	corporal
recapitulate	impede	pedant	corporation
	expedition	pedantic	
	podiatry		
	podium		

SORT 34 GREEK ROOT -*ONYM*-; AND LATIN ROOT -*GEN*-

This sort discusses the root -*onym*-, which means "name," and -*gen*-, which means "birth" or "beginning."

Background Information

The root -*onym*- occurs in a number of words. *Anti* + *onym* is, literally, "opposite name." Here the *i* is dropped in the prefix *anti*-; this occurred in the original Greek. Point out to students that in words created in modern English, such as *antioxidant*, the *i* remains before a vowel. Dropping of the *i* also occurred with *patronymic*. Ask students if they can recall two other words recently studied that have the same root, -*patr*- (e.g., *patriarch*, *patriarchy*), and if they can then infer the meaning of *patronymic* (literally, "relating to one's father's name"). A third word that drops the *i* is *eponym*, which comes from classical Greek and is composed of *epi*- (after) + *onym*, literally "named after." *Eponym* provides an excellent opportunity to discuss a number of words created from names such as *boycott, bloomers,* and *guillotine* (see Table 8-10 in *Words Their Way*). Students may well be familiar with *pseudonym*, a "false name" under which someone writes.

Acro means "summit" or "height"; it can also mean the "tip" or "beginning" of something. The latter is the sense that it has in the word *acronym*. An *acronym* is a word made from the beginning letters of a name: LASER, for example, comes from "*l*ight *a*mplification *by* *s*timulated *e*mission of *r*adiation."

Homonym, literally "same name," refers to words such as *table* (*table* at which people eat, water *table*) and *bank* (where you put your money, river *bank*). Contrast *homonym* with *heteronym*, literally "different name," as in *dove* ("The *dove* is associated with peace" versus "He *dove* into the bag of chips") and *tear* ("A *tear* ran down his face" versus "There is a *tear* in her bag").

The root -*gen*- occurs in a surprisingly large number of words, and although its meaning has extended metaphorically, it usually retains at its core the sense of "beginning." We speak of the *genesis* of an idea or event (as well as the first book of the Old Testament and the Torah, something students often haven't realized). The root -*gen*- has this straightforward meaning in *generator* and *regenerate*. A *progenitor* is a direct ancestor (one who begins before), and this word applies not only to hereditary issues but also to ideas, art, and so forth, as in the *progenitor* of a type of music. The related word *progeny* refers to offspring, literally or metaphorically, as with the *progeny* of an artistic movement begun by an earlier artist. *Genetic* derives from *gene*, which also refers to "beginning."

The root -*gen*- has extended in its meaning to refer to "kind," as with *generic*, which refers to a *general* category; *genre*, which refers to a class or type of literature, music, or art, and so forth.

Demonstrate

Have students work in pairs to group the words by root, then discuss their possible meanings. Students will have at least heard most of the words, though they may be uncertain about their meanings. Students may check these words in their dictionaries.

-onym-	*-gen-*
synonym	**generator**
antonym	genesis
anonymous	progenitor
patronymic	generic
pseudonym	genre
eponym	regenerate
acronym	progeny
homonym	genetic
	gene
	hydrogen

Extend

Hunt for other words that have *pseudo* in them. (*Pseudoword* is a good example!)

CUMULATIVE CHECK 5

Ask students to spell and define the following words:

1. allegiance	2. modality	3. adjudicate
4. benevolent	5. malicious	6. bureaucracy
7. hierarchy	8. aristocracy	9. equanimity
10. omniscient	11. recapitulate	12. pedagogy
13. progenitor	14. generic	15. genre

-*jud*-	-*leg*-	-*leg*-	-*biblio*-	-*mod*-
prejudice		**legalistic**		**legible**
bibliography		**moderate**		adjudicate
legislate		legend		bibliophile
allegiance		mode		judiciary
bibliomania		legion		biblical
bibliotheca		modern		allege
modernity		allegation		modality
accommodate		privilege		

-bene-	*-mal-*	*ante-*	*post-*

benefit	malfunction	antebellum
postdate	beneficial	malevolent
benefactor	ante meridiem	dismal
antedate	post meridiem	postbellum
malicious	malaria	malcontent
anterior	antemortem	malefactor
malice	postmortem	maladroit
benevolent	malfeasance	posterior

SORT 31 Greek and Latin Elements: Government (-*crat*/-*cracy*, -*archy*/ -*arch*-)

-*cracy*	-*crat*	-*archy*	-*arch*-
autocracy	**autocrat**	**monarchy**	
monarch	democracy	democrat	
oligarchy	technocrat	oligarch	
plutocrat	matriarch	anarchist	
aristocracy	patriarchy	hierarchy	
hierarchical	bureaucracy	bureaucrat	
matriarchy	anarchy	aristocrat	
technocracy	plutocracy	patriarch	

SORT 32 Greek and Latin Elements: Amount (*magni-*, *macro-*, *poly-*, *equ-*, *omni-*)

magni-	*macro-*	*poly-*	*equ-*	*omni-*

magnificent		**macroscopic**		**polysyllabic**
equator		**omnipotent**		equilateral
polygon		magnification		omnivore
equatorial		omniscient		polymath
polysemous		magnitude		equitable
equation		equivalent		polytechnic
polyglot		equanimity		
omnidirectional			macroeconomics	

SORT 33 Greek and Latin Elements: Related to the Body (-*cap*-, -*ped*-/ -*pod*-, -*ped*-, -*corp*-)

-*cap*-	-*ped*-/-*pod*-	-*ped*-	-*corp*-
decapitate	**pedestrian**		**pediatric**
corpse	capitol		pedicure
pedagogy	corps		capital
pedestal	pedagogue		corpulent
captivity	centipede		pediatrician
corporal	recapitulate		impede
pedant	corporation		expedition
pedantic	podiatry		podium

-*onym*-	-*gen*-	
synonym	**generator**	antonym
genesis	anonymous	progenitor
patronymic	generic	genre
pseudonym	regenerate	progeny
eponym	genetic	acronym
gene	homonym	hydrogen

Words Their Way: Word Sorts for Derivational Relations Spellers © 2006 by Prentice-Hall, Inc.

SORTS 35–43

Greek and Latin Elements III

NOTES FOR THE TEACHER

Many of the Greek and Latin elements explored in sorts 35–43 are more "connotative" than literal in their function. As with a number of the roots in sorts 29–34, however, it may often still be helpful to walk through the literal meaning of the combination of these elements, as students may then understand and appreciate how the meaning has evolved. When students understand the finer shades of meaning and connotation that elements at this level reflect, they are very well prepared to dissect, analyze, and reconstruct unfamiliar words they will encounter in their reading and study across a wide range of content domains. Importantly, the types of attention given to word study at this level are similar to the types of thinking required for understanding and acquiring another language.

In many instances reference is made to the Indo-European root to which a particular Latin root may be traced. Although exploration of Indo-European roots is not emphasized in these sorts, the occasional mention here offers students an intriguing glimpse into more advanced word study. Now that it is easier to access the Dictionary of Indo-European Roots either on CD or online (**http://www.bartleby.com/61/IEroots.html**), the potential for more students to pursue word etymology is promising.

SORT 35   GREEK AND LATIN ROOTS (-*VOC*-, -*LING*-, -*MEM*-, -*PSYCH*-)

The roots in this sort refer to language or to the mind: -*ling*- means "language"; -*voc*- means "voice"; -*mem*- means "mind"; and -*psych*- means "mind" or "mental."

Background Information

Begin with -*voc*- and the words in which the meaning of the root and its function are straightforward: *vocal* (characterizing or having to do with the voice) and *vocabulary*. Share with the students that *advocate* literally means "speaking to" or "toward" something, which is what an *advocate* does or what you do when you *advocate* for someone. *Provoke,* literally meaning "to call forth," has taken on a metaphorical meaning; to bring forth anger, for example.

You may wish to discuss the spelling-meaning relationship among the words *provoke/provocation/provocative,* noting the sound changes across the words. *Invoke* literally means "to call in" or, more metaphorically, to call upon another for help. In the related words *provocation* and *invocation* the spelling of *voc* changes; in English spelling, *-oce* is not an allowable word-final spelling pattern, but *-oke* is.

Remind students of the words *bilingual* and *monolingual;* what, then, does *multilingual* mean? The root *-ling-* refers to "language," but point out to the students that it originally meant "tongue" in Latin; the extension to language more generally was quite natural. Words with the *-ling-* root offer some good possibilities for exploration: A *linguist* is one who studies language, and a *sociolinguist* studies how language is used in a social context. A *linguaphile* is one who loves language; remind students of the *phile* words they learned in sort 29 (*phile* refers to "having a strong preference for, loving"). After discussing these *-ling-* words, ask the students why they think *linguini* has the *-ling-* root. You may need to remind them of the original Latin meaning for *ling,* "tongue"; so the meaning of *linguini,* therefore, returns us to "having to do with the tongue"! You may use this opportunity to remind students that English shares a number of roots with other languages, and *linguini* is a great example of this.

The root *-mem-* is fairly straightforward. *Memory* has to do, obviously, with the mind. *Remembrance,* of course, is derived from *remember*—literally, bringing the mind "back." *Commemorate* has to do with honoring the memory of someone—remembering "with" (*com*) others. Discuss *immemorial* by introducing this sentence: "Since time *immemorial,* people have said that dogs are humans' best friend." Discuss how the meaning "without memory" literally refers to a time beyond anyone's memory. (Note: A spelling hint for the *-mem-* words. Often students are uncertain whether to double the *m* in words such as *commemorate* and *immemorial.* Remind them that they should always first think of such words in terms of the base word or root—*memory* or *mem*—and prefixes that are added to the base or root.)

The root *-psych-* provides a good opportunity to return to Table 8-8, "Words from Greek and Roman Myths and Legends" in *Words Their Way.* Discuss some other words that have come from these stories. *Psyche,* the young Greek woman who fell in love with Eros, became the personification of the soul. Discuss with students how *-psych-* then came to mean "mind." (This may also be the time to acknowledge the *Eros-erotic* link, if your students notice it.) In discussing *psychiatry,* ask your students if they recall another *-iatry* word recently studied (*podiatry*). *-iatry* means "healing," so what is the literal meaning of *psychiatry*? Ask students if they recall another word, also recently studied, that has to do with *linguistics* (*sociolinguistics*); *psycholinguistics* thus refers to the study of how the mind influences the development of language. Share with students that *pathology* is the study of disease, usually a *particular* disease. What, then, might *psychopathology* be the study of?

Demonstrate

Have students work in pairs to group the words by roots, then discuss their possible meanings. Students will have at least heard most words, though they may be uncertain about their meanings. Students may check these words in their dictionaries.

-voc-	*-ling-*	*-mem-*	*-psych-*
vocal	**linguist**	**memory**	**psychology**
vocalic	linguaphile	memorial	psychiatry
vocabulary	sociolinguist	remembrance	psychopathology
advocate	linguini	commemorate	psycholinguistics
invoke	multilingual	memorandum	
invocation		immemorial	
provoke			
provocation			
provocative			

SORT 36   GREEK SUFFIXES (-*PHOBIA*/-*PHOBIC*, -*INE*, -*ITIS*, -*IDE*)

These suffixes apply to a large number of words, particularly in the physical sciences: -*phobia*/-*phobic*, which means "fear"; -*ine*, which means "like" or "chemical substance"; -*itis*, which means "disease of" or "inflammation of"; and -*ide*, which means "chemical substance."

Demonstrate

These suffixes may best be explored through an explicit walk-through. First, discuss the meanings of each of the suffixes in the boldfaced words. After discussing the meaning of *claustrophobia*, for example, tell the students that the root -*claustr*- comes from the Latin word for an enclosed space—the same Latin word later generated the words *cloister* and *closet*. The suffixes -*phobia*/-*phobic* come from *Phobos*, the name of the Greek god of fear, as well as the name of one of the moons of Mars. (Note: If students notice that -*ia* and -*ic* are also suffixes, good! They have the meaning "relating to," so they will understand that -*phobia* and -*phobic* both literally mean "relating to fear.") The suffix -*ine* can mean "of or relating to," as in *serpentine*, *crystalline*, and *medicine*, or can indicate a chemical substance.

Discuss which of the words in this sort fall into the category of "I've heard of it, but am not sure of the meaning." You may wish to discuss some of these words or simply direct the students to look them up and study the etymology, then discuss with the rest of the group how each word has come to have its current meaning. Until students study chemistry and biology, understanding that the suffix -*ide* refers to a chemical substance is sufficient. Students may know that *arachnophobia* means "a fear of spiders," but may not know the myth of Arachne. The root -*xeno*- comes from Greek and means "stranger"; illustrate its meaning with the sentence "During the war the nation was gripped by a wave of *xenophobia*."

-*phobia*/-*phobic*	-*ine*	-*itis*	-*ide*
claustrophobia	**adrenaline**	**tonsillitis**	**monoxide**
arachnophobia	alkaline	laryngitis	peroxide
technophobic	medicine	arthritis	bromide
xenophobia	chlorine	sinusitis	hydroxide
	crystalline		fluoride
	figurine		chloride
	antihistamine		
	serpentine		

Extend

Generate other words that share spelling/meaning relationships with the words in the sort; for example, *arthritis/arthritic*; *tonsillectomy* (literally, -*tomy* (cutting) + -*ec*- (out) of the tonsils). (Note: A link with Indo-European can be mentioned at this point. *Arth* comes from the Indo-European word for "joint"; this Indo-European root is still evident in the word *arm*.)

SORT 37   GREEK AND LATIN ROOTS (-*PATH*-, -*SENS*-/-*SENT*-, -*MED*-/-*MEDI*-, -*SOL*-, -*SEC*-/-*SECT*-)

This sort discusses -*sens*-/-*sent*-, meaning "sense"; -*med*-/-*medi*-, meaning "heal"; -*sol*-, meaning "alone"; and -*sec*-/-*sect*-, "to cut."

Demonstrate

As with the previous sort, this sort provides an excellent opportunity to walk through the words and elements explicitly.

Have students sort the words by root. Then, discuss the meaning of each. Remind students that in sort 35 they learned about the word *psychopathology*, in which the root *-path-* referred to "disease." In the word *sympathy*, does the root still mean "disease"? This root is a good example of metaphorical extension: The original root in Greek meant "suffering," but became extended to mean *disease*, and *feeling* or *emotion*, and it is in the latter sense that it functions in words such as *sympathy*, *empathy*, and *pathos*. Mention that *sympathy/sympathetic* and *empathy/empathetic* are often confused: You are *empathetic* if you truly feel like someone else is feeling and you have experienced what they are experiencing; you are *sympathetic* if you feel sorry for them. Have students dissect and discuss the literal meanings of *apathy*, *telepathy*, and *antipathy* ("without feeling," "feeling from far away," "feeling against").

Interestingly, *-med-/-medi-* (to heal) came from the same Indo-European root that had to do with "measuring," and literally means "to take appropriate measures." When a doctor attempts to heal someone, she literally "takes appropriate measures." Have students dissect *remedy* and *remedial* (to heal again). *Medevac* is a "blended" form constructed from *medical* and *evacuation*. The root *-sens-/-sent-* refers to "feeling" and has evolved to refer to "opinion" as well. With this in mind, have students analyze the *-sens-/-sent-* words.

After discussing the meaning of *solitary*, have students suggest the possible meaning of the root *-sol-*. Extend this discussion to the other *-sol-* words. With *-sec-/-sect-*, provide the meaning of the root and have students suggest how the root might function in the words to result in the meaning of each.

-path-	*-sens-/-sent-*	*-med-/-medi-*	*-sol-*	*-sec-/-sect-*
sympathy	**sensor**	**medicinal**	**solitary**	**dissect**
apathy	sentient	remedy	soliloquy	bisect
telepathy	sentiment	remedial	solitaire	insect
antipathy	dissent	medevac	desolate	intersect
empathy			solitude	sectarian
pathos				

Extend

Apathy and *telepathy* are nouns. What are their adjectival forms? (*apathetic, telepathic*) How does the sound change across these words?

SORT 38   LATIN ROOTS (-VER-/-VERS-/-VERT-, -VEN-/-VENT-, -JUNCT-, -SPIR-)

This sort discusses the Latin roots *-ver-/-vers-/-vert-* meaning "to turn"; *-ven-/-vent-*, meaning "to come"; *-junct-*, meaning "to join"; and *-spir-*, meaning "to breathe."

Demonstrate

Have students sort the words according to the root in each. Follow up by having students discuss, in pairs, how they think the word parts combine to produce the meaning of each word. Have students check the inferred meaning of each root by looking up challenging words in the dictionary.

In most of the *-spir-* words, the combination of the root and affixes results in a more metaphorical or connotative meaning. *Expire,* for example, literally means "to breathe out," but for the last time. *Conspire,* literally meaning "to breathe with," reflects a close relationship between individuals (*conspiracy*).

You may also have the students sort words into base word/derived word pairs: *invert/inversion, convene/convention,* and so forth. As with sort 28, this sort affords you the opportunity to discuss why the spelling of the root changes: The phonology or pronunciation exerts an influence. For example, when the noun *conversion* was formed from the verb *convert* it was easier to say "converzhun" than "convershun," and so the spelling had to reflect this pronunciation. Note, however, that *most* of the time the root's spelling *does* remain the same: *ver.* In some instances, as in *receive/reception,* the spelling of the root changes significantly. This, too, is because the phonological rules had to be honored in the spelling of the words: We don't say "receivshun."

On an etymological note, the literal meaning of *version* refers to the different "turns" or perspectives in recounting or telling a story.

-ver-/-vers-/-vert-	*-ven-/-vent-*	*-junct-*	*-spir-*
avert	**circumvent**	**conjunction**	**expire**
version	convention	juncture	respiration
convert	convene	adjunct	inspiration
invert	intervention	junction	aspiration
advertise	intervene		conspire
vertigo			transpire
conversion			
aversion			
inversion			

SORT 39   PREFIXES (*INTRA-*, *INTER-*, *INTRO-*)

The prefixes *intra-*, meaning "within"; *inter-*, meaning "between" or "among"; and *intro-*, meaning "in" or "inward" are quite common in English vocabulary. In this sort, these prefixes are examined as they occur in known as well as unknown words.

Demonstrate

Have students sort the words by prefix, and discuss what they think each prefix means. Then do a subsort of words that they know, have heard or seen, or do not know. Explore those about which they have heard or that they do not know.

Ask students what root they see in *introvert* and *introversion.* If necessary, remind them of the *vert/vers* words they examined in sort 38. Both of these words literally mean "to turn inward." Ask also about *intervene*; they examined this root in sort 38 as well. If you *intervene* to stop an argument, you literally "come in between" the parties.

Tell the students that *intercept* contains the root *-cept-*, meaning "to take." Do they see how the prefix and root result in the meaning of "to take in between"?

Recall from sort 24 that the root *-spect-* means "to look"; so if someone engages in *introspection*, they literally "look inward."

Students are familiar with the word *intramural,* but usually have not analyzed it. Ask them to define *mural,* then either tell them or have them look up the Latin meaning of *mural* ("wall"). The word *intramural* has the literal meaning "within the wall," so *intramural* sports are, understandably, within the walls of the same school; *intermural* sports are "between" the walls of different schools.

Inter alia is a Latin phrase meaning "among other things," as in, for example, the sentence "That point of view is, *inter alia*, irrelevant." Ask the students what word, meaning "other," they are reminded of (*alien, alias*).

intra-	*inter-*	*intro-*
intramural	**intermural**	**introvert**
intravenous	interregnum	introversion
intragalactic	international	introspection
intracellular	interpersonal	
intrapersonal	inter alia	
intrastate	intercept	
intranational	internet	

SORT 40   LATIN ROOTS (-*PRESS*-, -*PURG*-, -*FUS*-, -*PEND*-, -*PET*-)

This sort examines -*press*-, which means "to press"; -*purg*-, which means "to cleanse"; -*fuse*-, which means "to pour"; -*pend*-, which means "to hang"; and -*pet*-, which means "to go toward" or "to seek or strive for." Students will know most of the words in this sort. The primary objective here is to understand how these particular roots contribute to the meaning of the words in which they occur.

Background Information

-*fus*- is perhaps most interesting in that its meaning ("pour") has become metaphorically extended in a large number of words. Have students analyze and discuss the literal meaning of each of the words (e.g., *transfusion* is literally "to pour across"; *effusive* is literally "to pour out," etc.). Ask students if *purge* reminds them of a very common word (*pure*). In Christian belief, *purgatory* is a place where the souls of those who have not died "in grace" must linger until they have atoned for, or "purged," their sins. -*pet*- is usually straightforward, although in the word *competitive* the original literal meaning of "to strive *with*" now has changed to the opposite meaning, "to strive against." (Interestingly, in Shakespeare's time it *did* mean "to work *with*.")

Demonstrate

Have students sort the words according to the root in each. Follow up by having students discuss, in pairs, how they think the word parts combine to produce the meaning of each word. Have students check the inferred meaning of each root by looking up challenging words in the dictionary.

-*press*-	-*purg*-	-*fus*-	-*pend*-	-*pet*-
compression	**purge**	**transfusion**	**pendulum**	**appetite**
oppression	expurgate	diffuse	suspend	repetition
suppress	purgatory	confuse	pendant	perpetual
expressive	Puritan	infusion	appendage	competitive
		effusive	perpendicular	
		fusion		
		profuse		

SORT 41 LATIN ROOTS (-POS-, -LOC-, -SIST-, -STA-/ -STAT-/-STIT-)

This sort discusses the Latin roots -pos-, meaning "to put or place"; -loc-, meaning "place"; -sist, meaning "to stand"; -sta-/-stat-/-stit-, meaning "to stand."

Background Information

-sist- and -sta-/-stat-/-stit- come from the original Indo-European root *sta*, meaning "to stand" or "to set up." Interestingly, just two letters of this root remain in some words, for example, the *st* in re*st*. The word *rest* literally means "to stand again," being composed of the prefix *re-* and the root -sta-. A striking number of words contain a part that originated with this Indo-European root.

This root provides a good opportunity to talk with students about how the meaning of a word evolves from the combination of the root and affixes that compose it. For example, if something is *constant* it continually "stands with"; *statistics* describe the "state" of things or "where they stand"—people, trends, weather, and so on. In Latin, *sist* means "to stand"; the words *insist* and *persistent*, for example, have the sense of standing firmly. A *constitution* is a document that "sets up" (*stit*) a nation; a *substitute* is someone or something that stands (*stit*) in place of (*sub*); and when someone is granted *restitution* they are literally "set (back) up," usually monetarily.

Demonstrate

Have students sort the words by root, and ask which ones they can guess the meaning of. -loc-, and possibly -pos-, will probably be the most obvious to them. Most of us don't realize that -sist- and -sta-/-stat-/-stit- are variants of the same root meaning "to stand." Engage the students in analyzing the words containing these roots and then checking them with the dictionary. This is a good opportunity to discuss the prefix *ob-*, meaning "against."

-pos-	*-loc-*	*-sist-*	*-sta-/-stat-*	*-stit-*
propose	**local**	**insistent**	**instability**	**constitution**
proposition	locale	persistent	stable	restitution
preposition	locality	insist	statistics	substitute
juxtaposition	locomotion	assist	obstacle	
expository	allocate		constant	
decomposition			establish	

Extend

Have students be on the lookout for for -sist- and -sta-/-stat-/-stit- in their reading and record examples in their vocabulary notebooks.

SORT 42 LATIN ROOTS (-DUCE/-DUCT-, -CED-/-CESS-/ -CEED)

These roots, -duce/-duct-, meaning "to lead"; and -ced-/-cess-/-ceed, meaning "to go," occur frequently and their spellings change depending on the words in which they occur.

Demonstrate

You may begin this sort with the words *introduce* and *introduction*, which were explored in sort 7 as part of the "*e*-drop + *-ion* or *-tion*" suffix. Have students discuss the literal meanings of *introduce* ("to lead in") and *introduction* ("the act or result of leading in"). Do they see how the meaning of each word has connotatively evolved into its present meaning? Continue by sorting the words by root.

-duce/-duct-	*-ced-/-cess-/-ceed*
induce	**proceed**
education	procession
educe	recede
induction	recession
deduce	exceed
deduction	precede
abduct	secede
abduction	secession
reduce	intercede
aqueduct	intercession
viaduct	succeed

Observe that *proceed*, *exceed*, and *succeed* are the only words in which the spelling of the root *-ced-* is *ceed*.

SORT 43   PREDICTABLE SPELLING CHANGES IN WORD ROOTS (-*CEIV*-/-*CEP*-, -*TAIN*/-*TEN*-, -*NOUNCE*/-*NUNC*-)

This sort examines the word roots *-ceiv-/-cep-*, meaning "to take"; *-tain/-ten-*, meaning "to hold"; and *-nounce/-nunc-*, meaning "to report."

Background Information

The words in this sort illustrate that the spelling in semantically related words can change, but when it does, it does so predictably. For example, when examining words one at a time one may question why the spelling of the root changes. This phenomenon was first explored in sort 28 and again in sort 38. In this sort, the spelling change is significant; but when the words are grouped in spelling-meaning families, students can see how this change is predictable. Adding suffixes to words such as *deceive*, *retain*, and *pronounce* changes the spelling in these words in a pattern that is predictable and applies to other words with these roots.

Demonstrate

Have students sort the words according to the root in each. Follow up by having students discuss, in pairs, how they think the word parts combine to produce the meaning of each word.

-ceiv-/-cep-	-tain/-ten-	-nounce/-nunc-
deceive	**retain**	**pronounce**
perceive	detain	renounce
preconceive	attain	denounce
deception	abstain	pronunciation
perception	sustain	renunciation
preconception	retention	denunciation
	detention	
	attention	
	abstention	
	sustenance	

Extend

Other words that you may share with the students are *abound/abundant, profound/profundity, redound/redundant, fund/foundation*. The rule of *"i* before *e* except after *c"* applies in the spelling of *deceive, perceive,* and *preconceive*.

CUMULATIVE CHECK 6

Ask students to spell and define the following words:

1. provocation
2. memorandum
3. adrenaline
4. laryngitis
5. empathy
6. dissect
7. intervene
8. aversion
9. introspection
10. expurgate
11. appendage
12. allocate
13. precede
14. secession
15. sustenance

-voc-	-ling-	-mem-	-psych-
vocal	**linguist**		**memory**
psychology	vocalic		linguaphile
memorandum	psychiatry		vocabulary
sociolinguist	memorial		immemorial
remembrance	advocate		invocation
psychopathology	linguini		provocative
psycholinguistics	provoke		multilingual
commemorate	invoke		provocation

Words Their Way: Word Sorts for Derivational Relations Spellers © 2006 by Prentice-Hall, Inc.

SORT 36   Greek Suffixes (-*phobia*/-*phobic*, -*ine*, -*itis*, -*ide*)

-*phobia*/ -*phobic*	-*ine*	-*itis*	-*ide*
claustrophobic	**adrenaline**	**tonsillitis**	
monoxide	chloride	alkaline	
antihistamine	laryngitis	peroxide	
technophobia	medicine	chlorine	
serpentine	crystalline	arthritis	
xenophobia	bromide	figurine	
hydroxide	sinusitis	fluoride	
arachnophobia			

SORT 37 Greek and Latin Roots (*-path-*, *-sens-/-sent-*, *-med-/-medi-*, *-sol-*, *-sec-/-sect-*)

-path-	*-sens-/ -sent-*	*-med-/ -medi-*	*-sol-*	*-sec-/ -sect-*
sympathy		**sensor**		**medicinal**
solitary		**dissect**		telepathy
sentient		remedy		soliloquy
bisect		apathy		sentiment
remedial		solitaire		insect
intersect		antipathy		dissent
medevac		desolate		sectarian
empathy		solitude		pathos

-ver-/-vers-/-vert-	-ven-/-vent-	-junct-	-spir-
avert	**circumvent**	**conjunction**	
expire	version	convention	
juncture	respiration	convert	
inversion	convene	adjunct	
inspiration	advertise	conspire	
vertigo	intervention	transpire	
aversion	intervene	invert	
conversion	aspiration	junction	

intra-	*inter-*	*intro-*
intramural	**intermural**	**introvert**
intravenous	intranational	intragalactic
international	introversion	intracellular
inter alia	intrapersonal	intercept
intrastate	interpersonal	internet
interregnum	introspection	

-*press*-	-*purg*-	-*fus*-	-*pend*-	-*pet*-
compression		**purge**		**transfusion**
pendulum		**appetite**		oppression
expurgate		diffuse		suspend
repetition		profuse		suppress
purgatory		confuse		pendant
perpetual		expressive		Puritan
infusion		appendage		competitive
perpendicular		fusion		effusive

SORT 41   Latin Roots (-pos-, -loc-, -sist-, -sta-/-stat-/-stit-)

-pos-	*-loc-*	*-sist-*	*-sta-/-stat-*	*-stit-*
propose		**local**		**insistent**
instability		**constitution**		proposition
locale		persistent		stable
restitution		preposition		locality
insist		statistics		locomotion
assist		juxtaposition		allocate
obstacle		substitute		establish
expository		decomposition		constant

SORT 42 Latin Roots (-*duce*/-*duct*-, -*ced*-/-*cess*-/-*ceed*)

-*duce*/-*duct*-		-*ced*-/-*cess*-/-*ceed*
induce	**proceed**	education
educe	procession	recede
induction	recession	deduce
exceed	deduction	precede
abduct	secede	abduction
secession	reduce	intercede
aqueduct	intercession	viaduct
succeed		

SORT 43 Predictable Spelling Changes (-*ceiv-*/-*cep-*, -*tain*/-*ten-*, -*nounce*/-*nunc-*)

-*ceiv-*/-*cep-*	-*tain*/-*ten-*	-*nounce*/-*nunc-*
deceive	**retain**	**pronounce**
deception	retention	pronunciation
perceive	perception	preconception
preconceive	detain	attention
detention	attain	abstention
abstain	sustain	sustenance
renounce	denounce	renunciation
		denunciation

SORTS 44-50

Advanced Spelling-Meaning Patterns

NOTES FOR THE TEACHER

The spelling-meaning patterns explored in sorts 44–50 address the types of errors that plague more advanced spellers: -ent/-ant and -ence/-ance uncertainties, confusion over -able/-ible, not knowing when to double the final consonant when adding inflectional endings to words such as *benefit*, and not recognizing the doubled consonants that reflect *assimilated prefixes*.

SORT 44   SUFFIXES (-ENT/-ENCE, -ANT/-ANCE) I

The relationship between -ent/-ence and -ant/-ance is powerful and straightforward. Students' understanding of this relationship, however, depends on considerable experience with these patterns and the words that represent them. Therefore, sorts 44 and 45 appear at this point in the scope and sequence rather than earlier.

Demonstrate

Have students sort the words by pairs; for example, align *confidence* with *confident* and *brilliance* with *brilliant*. Tell the students that by arranging the words this way they will find a clue to the -ent/-ence and -ant/-ance puzzle.

The key to understanding these suffixes is this: If you know how to spell one word that ends in -ent and -ence or -ant and -ance, then you can figure out how to spell the word about which you're uncertain. For example, if you are uncertain whether a spelling is *dependant* or *dependent* but you know how to spell the word *independence*, then *independence* is your clue to the spelling of *dependent*: -ent and -ence words go together, and -ant and -ance words go together.

-ent	-ence	-ant	-ance
confident	**confidence**	**brilliant**	**brilliance**
dependent	dependence	fragrant	fragrance
resident	residence	dominant	dominance
different	difference	abundant	abundance
obedient	obedience		
excellent	excellence		
prominent	prominence		
patient	patience		

Extend

Have students determine which pattern, *-ent/-ence* or *-ant/-ance,* appears to be the most frequent. (It's *-ent/-ence.*)

SORT 45   SUFFIXES (*-ENT/-ENCE, -ANT/-ANCE*) II

This sort confirms the understandings developed in the previous sort, and clearly illustrates which pattern is more frequent.

-ant	*-ance*	*-ent*	*-ence*
irrelevant	**irrelevance**	**imminent**	**imminence**
abundant	abundance	impertinent	impertinence
defiant	defiance	adolescent	adolescence
		inconvenient	inconvenience
		incoherent	incoherence
		inherent	inherence
		adherent	adherence
		iridescent	iridescence

Extend

Have students suggest as many words as they can that are related to the words in this sort. For example, point out *cohesive* (*incoherent/incoherence*) and *adhesive* (*adherent/adherence*). The "Defiance or Patience?" game in Chapter 8 and its variations is helpful at this point.

SORT 46   SUFFIXES (*-ABLE/-IBLE*)

Chapter 8 in *Words Their Way* presents a sequence of sorts that helps develop a comprehensive understanding of the *-able/-ible* phenomenon. This sort develops the core understanding that, when adding this suffix to a base word, it usually is spelled *-able;* when adding to a word root, it is usually spelled *-ible.*

Demonstrate

Have the students sort the *-able* words and the *-ible* words in separate categories. Then, ask them to examine each category to see if they notice a pattern: When is this suffix spelled *-able* and when is it spelled *-ible*? (*-able* is usually added to base words; *-ible* is usually added to word roots.)

-able	*-ible*
dependable	credible
profitable	audible
predictable	legible
perishable	plausible
laughable	indelible
punishable	intangible
adaptable	irascible
attainable	feasible
cherishable	compatible
decipherable	combustible
sustainable	

SORT 47 ADDING -*ABLE*: WHEN DO YOU KEEP THE *E*?

Demonstrate

Have students sort the words into two columns: Words in which the *e* is dropped before adding -*able*, and those in which the *e* is kept. The key point to understand is that the *e* is kept when omitting it would result in a change in pronunciation. For example, in *noticeable*, the *c* would become "hard"; in *manageable*, the *g* would also become hard.

Drop *e*	Keep *e*
farmable	noticeable
unnamable	manageable
consumable	danceable
excusable	exchangeable
resumable	knowledgeable
undesirable	balanceable
indivisible	pronounceable
confusable	replaceable
pleasurable	salvageable
opposable	
reusable	
invisible	

The sorts in Activity 8-15 of *Words Their Way* expand on the -*able*/-*ible* phenomenon and will be a good follow-up to sorts 46 and 47.

SORT 48 ACCENT AND DOUBLING

This sort is illustrated in a teacher script in Chapter 8 of *Words Their Way*.

Background Information

It is helpful to share the story about Noah Webster's influence at this point (see Chapter 8). When he wrote the first dictionary of American English in 1828 he wanted to distinguish American English from British English. In addition to omitting the *u* in words such as *honour* and *colour* and reversing the *re* in *theatre* and *centre*, he changed the rules for "doubling" final consonants. In British English, the final consonant is almost always doubled (*benefitting, levelled*), but not (after 1828) in American English!

Demonstrate

Have students sort the words into two columns. In the first column the final consonant is doubled before adding -*ed* or -*ing*; in the second it is not. If students are unsure about the pattern, ask them to think about accent or stress. Ask students about the base words in the first column. Does the accent fall on the last syllable of the base word? (Yes.) What about the base words in the second column? Does the accent fall on the last syllable? (No.) Does that give them a clue? The generalization that applies here is "If the accent in the base word falls on the final syllable, then double the final consonant before adding the suffix. If the accent does not fall on the last syllable, do not double."

Double	Do Not Double
omitted	**orbited**
propellant	benefiting
compelling	leveled
occurred	piloting
preferred	preference
deferred	deference
concurring	modeling
conferred	libeled
committed	quarreled
appellant	referent
repellant	conference
referred	editing
abhorrent	

Extend

Share with the students that *travelling*, for example, is now equally acceptable with *traveling* and that they will see these spellings in books published in Great Britain and the rest of the British Commonwealth. Ask students to think about the base of *appellant* and *repellant*; these are instances in which the spelling of the base changes (*appeal, repeal*).

SORT 49   PREFIX ASSIMILATION: THE PREFIX *IN-*

Sorts 49 and 50 address assimilated or "absorbed" prefixes. In sort 49, the prefixes are attached to base words; in sort 50, they are attached to word roots. In order to understand this phenomenon, it is helpful to share the information presented in the *Background Information* section as part of the demonstration. An excellent illustration of a teacher guiding students to an understanding of this phenomenon may be found on the *Words Their Way* Video.

Demonstrate

Have students sort words according to the spelling of the prefix: *in-, im-, il-,* and *ir-*. Discuss the meaning of a few of the words: *Incorrect* means "not correct," *immobile* means "not mobile," and so forth. (In the words *inform* and *indent* the prefix does not, of course, mean "not"; instead, it has the meaning of "into.") Explain to students how they have known about the meaning and function of the prefix *in-* for quite a long time. Now the students will explore why the spelling of the prefix *in-* changes, even though the prefix keeps the same meaning.

Ask the students to look at the words in the *im-, il-,* and *ir-* columns. Do they see any clues as to why the spelling changes? Students usually notice the spelling of the first letter in the base words. In the *in-* column, however, why *doesn't* the spelling change? Have the students discuss this for a few moments. Occasionally a student *will* in fact come up with the explanation; if they remain stumped, however, then proceed as follows. (See also the teacher explanation in *Words Their Way*, Chapter 8.) Ask the students to try pronouncing several of the words in the *im-, il-,* and *ir-* columns *without* the spelling change in *in-*: *inmobile, inlegal, inregular*. Discuss how that feels odd or awkward—the tongue has to make a rapid change from the /n/ sound to the sound at the beginning of each word. Tell the students that this same awkwardness in pronunciation occurred in Latin over two thousand years ago; so over time, the sound of /n/ became assimilated or "absorbed" into the sound at the beginning of the word to which *in-* was attached, and eventually the spelling changed to reflect this assimilation. In most words in the *in-* column, the pronunciation is not as awkward. A student may note that *incorrect* is a bit hard to say: Why isn't it *iccorect*? Someday it may be—though you may wish to point out that the spelling system has changed far less since the printing press was invented, because the printed standard has tended to conserve existing spellings and spelling patterns.

in-	*im-*	*il-*	*ir-*
incorrect	**immobile**	**illegible**	**irreplaceable**
inactive	immoral	illegal	irremovable
inescapable	immeasurable	illiterate	irrational
incapable	immature	illogical	irresponsible
innumerable	immortal	illegitimate	irrefutable
inform			irreducible
indent			

Extend

Several of these words include *-able/-ible.* You may wish to review these suffixes with these words.

SORT 50   PREFIX ASSIMILATION: THE PREFIXES *IN-*, *COM-*, *AD-*, AND *SUB-*

Most words in this sort are composed of prefixes and word roots, though a few such as *immaterial* and *immigrant* are exceptions. Students have already explored the prefixes *in-*, *com-*, and *sub-*; *ad-* was addressed in sort 29.

Background Information

The same historical process applies to these words as to the words in sort 49. Students continue to develop their understanding of this process when they try to pronounce, for example, the following: *comlide, adtractive, subpression.*

in-	*com-*	*ad-*	*sub-*
immaterial	**collide**	**attractive**	**suppression**
immigrant	corrode	attachment	supportable
immense	commit	accountant	suffix
imminent	colleague	arrange	
immune	correlate	aggressive	
		aggregate	
		affiliate	
		affix	
		appended	
		appetite	

Extend

Sort 50 offers opportunities to review word roots, for example *-port-* (sort 24), *-tract-* and *-gress-* (sort 26), *-pend-* (sort 40), and *-mit-* (sort 27). You may wish to compare and contrast word pairs such as *collide/collision*. Point out *erode/erosion, commit/commission, elide/elision;* this helps to consolidate students' understanding of when consonants are doubled at the juncture of prefix and root. Examine the word *accommodate*, which is often misspelled. *Accommodate* contains two prefixes (*ad-* and *com-*) added to the root *-mod-*, which accounts for the double letters (*cc* and *mm*).

CUMULATIVE CHECK 7

Ask students to spell and define the following words:

1. obedience	2. irrelevance	3. adolescence
4. credible	5. attainable	6. salvageable
7. undesirable	8. repellant	9. benefiting
10. conference	11. innumerable	12. illegitimate
13. irrational	14. correlate	15. aggressive

-ent	-ence	-ant	-ance
confident	**confidence**		**brilliant**
brilliance	dependent		abundant
resident	fragrant		dependence
abundance	residence		fragrance
different	dominant		obedience
excellence	difference		dominance
obedient	patient		prominent
prominence	excellent		patience

-ant	-ance	-ent	-ence
irrelevant	**irrelevance**		**imminent**
imminence	impertinence		incoherent
inherent	adolescence		abundant
abundance	inconvenience		impertinent
adolescent	incoherence		defiant
iridescent	inconvenient		iridescence
defiance	inherence		adherence
adherent			

Words Their Way: Word Sorts for Derivational Relations Spellers © 2006 by Prentice-Hall, Inc.

-able	-ible	
dependable	**credible**	profitable
audible	predictable	legible
perishable	plausible	laughable
indelible	punishable	intangible
adaptable	irascible	attainable
combustible	cherishable	feasible
decipherable	compatible	sustainable

drop final *e*		keep final *e*
farmable	**noticeable**	unnamable
danceable	exchangeable	manageable
excusable	knowledgeable	consumable
reusable	balanceable	resumable
confusable	pronounceable	undesirable
opposable	pleasurable	replaceable
invisible	salvageable	indivisible

SORT 48   Accent and Doubling

double		do not double
omitted	**orbited**	propellant
benefiting	compelling	leveled
occurred	piloting	preferred
preference	conferred	deference
concurring	libeled	committed
quarreled	appellant	referent
repellent	conference	deferred
editing	abhorrent	modeling

Words Their Way: Word Sorts for Derivational Relations Spellers © 2006 by Prentice-Hall, Inc.

in-	*im-*	*il-*	*ir-*

incorrect	immobile	illegible
irreplaceable	inactive	immoral
irremovable	illegal	incapable
immeasurable	illiterate	irrational
irresponsible	illogical	immature
irrefutable	irregular	irreducible
illegitimate	immortal	inescapable
innumerable	inform	indent

Words Their Way: Word Sorts for Derivational Relations Spellers © 2006 by Prentice-Hall, Inc.

in-	*com-*	*ad-*	*sub-*
immaterial	**collide**		**attractive**
suppression	appended		immigrant
attachment	supportable		commit
immense	accountant		suffix
colleague	imminent		arrange
aggressive	correlate		aggregate
immune	affiliate		affix
appetite	corrode		

Appendix

Blank Template

Word Work at Home

Word Sort Corpus (numbers indicate the sort in which the words appear)

Blank Sort Template

Words Their Way: Word Sorts for Derivational Relations Spellers © 2006 by Prentice-Hall, Inc.

Word Work At Home

Name _____ Date _____

Cut apart your words and sort them first. Then write your words below under a key word.

_____

_____

_____

_____

_____

_____

_____

_____

_____

_____

What did you learn about words from this sort?

_____

_____

_____

On the back of this paper write the same key words you used above. Ask someone to shuffle your word cards and call them aloud as you write them into categories. Look at each word as soon as you write it. Correct it if needed.

Check off what you did and ask a parent to sign below.
_____ Sort the words again in the same categories you did in school.
_____ Write the words in categories as you copy the words.
_____ Do a no-peeking sort with someone at home.
_____ Write the words into categories as someone calls them aloud.
_____ Find more words in your reading that have the same sound and/or pattern. Add them to the categories on the back.
                    Signature of Parent _____

---

abduct	42	antedate	30	aversion	38	circumvent	38
abduction	42	antemortem	30	avert	38	claustrophobia	36
abhorrent	48	anterior	30	balanceable	47	cleaner	3
abrupt	26	antihistamine	36	barometer	22	cleanest	3
abstain	43	antipathy	37	benediction	25	clinic	6
abstention	43	antonym	34	benefactor	30	clinician	6
abundance	44	apathy	37	beneficial	30	colleague	50
abundant	44	appellant	48	benefit	30	collide	50
academic	18	appendage	40	benefiting	48	column	9
academy	18	appended	50	benevolent	30	columnist	9
acclaim	16	appetite	40, 50	biblical	29	combination	12
acclamation	16	aqueduct	42	bibliography	29	combine	12
accommodate	29	arachnophobia	36	bibliomania	29	combustible	46
accountant	50	aristocracy	31	bibliophile	29	comedian	15
acronym	34	aristocrat	31	bibliotheca	29	comedy	15
adaptable	46	arrange	50	bicameral	20	commemorate	35
adherence	45	arthritis	36	biceps	20	commit	50
adherent	45	artifact	28	biennial	20	committed	48
adjudicate	29	artifice	17	bilingual	20	compatible	46
adjunct	38	artificial	17	bimonthly	20	compelling	48
admiration	11	ascribe	28	binary	20	compete	11
admire	11	aspiration	38	biography	22	competition	11
admission	8	assert	6	biology	22	competitive	40
admit	8	assertion	6	biorhythms	22	compose	11
adolescence	45	assist	41	bisect	20, 37	composition	11
adolescent	45	assume	16	biweekly	20	compression	40
adopt	6	assumption	16	bomb	9	conceive	16
adoption	6	athlete	10	bombard	9	conception	16
adrenaline	36	athletic	10	bountiful	4	conclude	8
advertise	38	attachment	50	breath	10	conclusion	8
advocate	35	attain	43	breathe	10	concurring	48
affiliate	50	attainable	46	breathless	4	condemn	9
affix	50	attention	43	brilliance	44	condemnation	9
afternoon	2	attentiveness	4	brilliant	44	conference	48
aftertaste	2	attract	26	bromide	36	conferred	48
afterthought	2	attractive	50	brutal	13	confess	5
afterword	2	audible	25, 46	brutality	13	confession	5
aggregate	50	audience	25	bureaucracy	31	confidence	44
aggression	26	audiology	25	bureaucrat	31	confident	44
aggressive	50	audiotape	25	capital	33	confusable	47
alkaline	36	audition	25	capitol	33	confuse	40
allegiance	29	auditorium	25	captivity	33	congratulate	7
allocate	41	auditory	25	centipede	33	congratulation	7
allude	8	autobiography	22	central	13	congress	5
allusion	8	autocracy	31	centrality	13	congressional	5
anarchist	31	autocrat	31	cherishable	46	conjunction	38
anarchy	31	autograph	22	chloride	36	conspiracy	11
anonymous	34	automobile	22	chlorine	36	conspire	11, 38
ante meridiem	30	autumn	9	circumscribe	28	constant	41
antebellum	30	autumnal	9	circumspect	24	constitution	41

consumable	47	deference	48	dissent	37	exchangeable	47
consume	16	deferred	48	distinct	5	exclaim	16
consumption	16	defiance	45	distinction	5	exclamation	16
contradict	25	define	11	distract	26	excusable	47
convene	38	definition	11	distrust	1	expedition	33
convention	38	deflect	27	diverse	18	expire	38
conversion	38	delightful	4	diversion	18	explain	16
convert	38	democracy	31	divert	18	explanation	16
copious	18	democrat	31	divide	8	explode	8
copy	18	demote	26	divine	11	explosion	8
corporal	33	demotion	26	divinity	11	export	24
corporation	33	denounce	43	division	8	expository	41
corps	33	denunciation	43	dominance	44	express	5
corpse	33	dependable	46	dominant	44	expression	5
corpulent	33	dependence	44	earlier	3	expressive	40
correlate	50	dependent	44	earliest	3	expurgate	40
corrode	50	deport	24	edict	25	extinct	5
cosmetic	17	design	9	editing	48	extinction	5
cosmetician	17	designate	9	education	42	facilitate	28
create	7	desolate	37	educe	42	facsimile	28
creation	7	detain	43	effusive	40	factory	28
credence	28	detect	5	egress	26	familiar	12
credible	28, 46	detection	5	eject	27	familiarity	12
crime	10	detention	43	elect	5	fancier	3
criminal	10	detract	26	election	5	fanciest	3
critic	17	diagnostic	6	emit	27	fanciful	4
criticize	17	diagnostician	6	emote	26	farmable	47
crummier	3	dictate	25	emoticon	26	feasible	46
crummiest	3	dictator	25	emotion	26	ferocious	14
crystalline	36	diction	25	empathy	37	ferocity	14
custodian	11	dictionary	25	emphasis	15	figurine	36
custody	11	difference	44	emphatic	15	flawless	4
danceable	47	different	44	emptier	3	flawlessness	4
decapitate	33	diffuse	40	emptiest	3	flexible	27
decathlete	23	digest	6	emptiness	4	fluoride	36
decathlon	23	digestion	6	eponym	34	forearm	2
deceive	43	digress	26	equanimity	32	forecourt	2
deception	43	diplomacy	18	equation	32	foreknowledge	2
decide	8	diplomat	18	equator	32	foreordain	2
decimal	23	diplomatic	18	equatorial	32	forethought	2
decimate	23	disclose	1	equilateral	32	forewarn	2
decipherable	46	discontinue	1	equitable	32	foreword	2
decision	8	discredit	28	equivalent	32	fraction	27
decomposition	41	disease	1	erupt	26	fractious	27
decorate	7	disengage	1	establish	41	fracture	27
decoration	7	disgraceful	4	eventual	13	fragile	12
deduce	42	dismal	30	eventuality	13	fragility	12
deduction	42	disorder	1	exceed	42	fragrance	44
defamatory	18	disrupt	26	excellence	44	fragrant	44
defame	18	dissect	37	excellent	44	friendliness	4

frugal	19	illustrative	15	injection	27	invocation	35
frugality	19	imitate	7	innumerable	49	invoke	35
fruitless	4	imitation	7	inscribe	28	Iran	14
fusion	40	immaterial	50	inscription	28	Iranian	14
gene	34	immature	49	insect	37	irascible	46
general	13	immeasurable	49	insert	6	iridescence	45
generality	13	immemorial	35	insertion	6	iridescent	45
generate	7	immense	50	insightful	4	irrational	49
generation	7	immigrant	50	insist	41	irreducible	49
generator	34	imminence	45	insistent	41	irrefutable	49
generic	34	imminent	45, 50	inspection	24	irregular	49
genesis	34	immobile	49	inspiration	38	irrelevance	45
genetic	34	immoral	49	instability	41	irremovable	49
genre	34	immortal	49	intangible	46	irreplaceable	49
geology	22	immune	19, 50	inter alia	39	irresponsible	49
geothermal	22	immunity	19	intercede	42	italicize	17
grateful	10	immunization	19	intercept	39	italics	17
gratitude	10	impede	14, 33	intercession	42	janitor	15
harmonious	15	impediment	14	intermural	39	janitorial	15
harmony	15	impertinence	45	international	39	Jefferson	14
harsher	3	impertinent	45	internet	39	Jeffersonian	14
harshest	3	import	24	interpersonal	39	judiciary	29
haste	9	importune	24	interregnum	39	junction	38
hasten	9	impose	14	interrupt	26	juncture	38
heliport	24	imposition	14	intersect	37	juxtaposition	41
hierarchical	31	impugn	18	intervene	38	kinder	3
hierarchy	31	inactive	49	intervention	38	kindest	3
historian	15	inaudible	25	intracellular	39	knowledgeable	47
history	15	incapable	49	intragalactic	39	labor	15
homonym	34	incoherence	45	intramural	39	laborious	15
humane	10	incoherent	45	intranational	39	laryngitis	36
humanity	10	inconvenience	45	intrapersonal	39	laudable	25
humid	14	inconvenient	45	intrastate	39	laughable	46
humidity	14	incorrect	49	intravenous	39	legal	12
hydrogen	34	incredible	28	introduce	7	legalistic	29
hydroxide	36	incredulous	28	introduction	7	legality	12
hyperactive	21	indelible	46	introspect	24	legend	29
hypercritical	21	indicate	7	introspection	39	legible	29, 46
hyperirritable	21	indication	7	introversion	39	legion	29
hyperventilate	21	indict	25	introvert	39	legislate	29
hypervigilant	21	individual	13	intrude	8	leveled	48
ignite	10	individuality	13	intrusion	8	libeled	48
ignition	10	indivisible	47	invade	8	linguaphile	35
illegal	49	induce	42	invasion	8	linguini	35
illegible	49	induction	42	invent	6	linguist	35
illegitimate	49	inescapable	49	invention	6	local	41
illiterate	49	infraction	27	inversion	38	locale	41
illogical	49	infusion	40	invert	38	locality	41
illustrate	7, 15	inherence	45	invitation	12	locomotion	41
illustration	7	inherent	45	invite	12	logic	6

logician	6	microcosm	21	national	10	patient	44
looseness	4	microfilm	21	natural	10	patriarch	31
macroeconomics	32	micrometer	22	nature	10	patriarchy	31
macroscopic	32	Micronesia	21	neutral	13	patronymic	34
magic	6	microphone	21	neutrality	13	pedagogue	33
magician	6	microscope	21	normal	13	pedagogy	33
magnification	32	microsurgery	21	normality	13	pedant	33
magnificent	32	mine	10	noticeable	47	pedantic	33
magnitude	32	mineral	10	notoriety	19	pedestal	33
major	15	misconduct	1	notorious	19	pedestrian	33
majority	15	misfortune	1	obedience	44	pediatric	33
maladroit	30	mislead	1	obedient	44	pediatrician	33
malaria	30	misplace	1	objection	27	pedicure	33
malcontent	30	mission	27	obsolescent	19	pendant	40
malefactor	30	misstep	1	obsolete	19	pendulum	40
malevolent	30	mistake	1	obstacle	41	pentad	23
malfeasance	30	mobile	12	occurred	48	pentagon	23
malfunction	30	mobility	12	office	17	pentangle	23
malice	30	modality	29	official	17	pentarchy	23
malicious	30	mode	29	officiate	17	pentathlete	23
manageable	47	modeling	48	oligarch	31	pentathlon	23
mandate	15, 28	moderate	29	oligarchy	31	perceive	43
mandatory	15	modern	29	omission	8	perception	43
maneuver	28	modernity	29	omit	8, 27	perimeter	22
manicure	28	moist	9	omitted	48	periscope	22
manual	28	moisten	9	omnidirectional	32	perishable	46
manufacture	28	monarch	31	omnipotent	32	permission	8
manure	28	monarchy	31	omniscient	32	permit	8, 27
manuscript	28	monolingual	20	omnivore	32	peroxide	36
massiveness	4	monologue	20	opportune	24	perpendicular	40
matriarch	31	monopod	20	opposable	47	perpetual	40
matriarchy	31	monopoly	20	oppose	12	persistent	41
medevac	37	monorail	20	opposition	12	personal	13
medicinal	37	monotone	20	oppress	5	personality	13
medicine	36	monotony	20	oppression	5, 40	perspective	24
mediocre	14	monoxide	36	optic	6	perspicacious	19
mediocrity	14	moral	13	optician	6	perspicacity	19
megabyte	21	morality	13	orbited	48	perspiration	12
megadose	21	multilingual	35	Oregon	14	perspire	12
megahit	21	murkier	3	Oregonian	14	phonics	22
megalopolis	21	murkiest	3	original	13	phonograph	22
megaphone	21	muscle	9	originality	13	phonology	22
memorandum	35	muscular	9	page	11	photograph	22
memorial	35	music	6	paginate	11	photosynthesis	22
memory	35	musical	13	Palestine	14	physicist	17
mental	13	musicality	13	Palestinian	14	physics	17
mentality	13	musician	6	paradigm	19	piloting	48
metal	12	narrate	15	paradigmatic	19	plausible	46
metallic	12	narrative	15	pathos	37	pleasurable	47
microbe	21	nation	10	patience	44	plutocracy	31

plutocrat	31	prescription	28	publicize	17	renounce	43
podiatry	33	preseason	2	pugnacious	18	renunciation	43
podium	33	preside	12	pugnacity	18	repackage	1
polar	19	president	12	punishable	46	repellant	48
polarity	19	presume	16	purgatory	40	repetition	40
politeness	4	presumption	16	purge	40	replaceable	47
political	17	presumptive	16	Puritan	40	report	24
politician	17	prewar	2	quadrangle	23	reproduce	7
politicize	17	priceless	4	quadrant	23	reproduction	7
polyglot	32	privilege	29	quadrennial	23	reptile	11
polygon	32	proceed	42	quadruped	23	reptilian	11
polymath	32	procession	42	quadruple	23	residence	44
polysemous	32	proclaim	16	quadruplets	23	resident	44
polysyllabic	32	proclamation	16	quarreled	48	resign	9
polytechnic	32	produce	7	quieter	3	resignation	9
portage	24	production	7	quietest	3	respectful	4
portfolio	24	profess	5	quintessence	23	respiration	38
possess	5	profession	5	quintessential	23	restitution	41
possession	5	profitable	46	quintuple	23	resumable	47
post meridiem	30	profuse	40	quintuplets	23	resume	16
postbellum	30	progenitor	34	reaction	1	resumption	16
postcolonial	2	progeny	34	reassure	1	retain	43
postdate	2, 30	progress	26	recapitulate	33	retention	43
posterior	30	prohibit	12	recede	42	retrospect	24
postmortem	30	prohibition	12	receive	16	reusable	47
postscript	28	project	27	reception	16	revise	10
postseason	2	projectile	27	receptive	16	revision	10
postwar	2	prominence	44	recession	42	rhapsodic	19
precede	42	prominent	44	reciprocal	19	rhapsody	19
precise	10	promote	26	reciprocate	19	rigid	15
precision	10	promotion	26	reciprocity	19	rigidity	15
precocious	14	pronounce	43	reclaim	16	rigorousness	4
precocity	14	pronounceable	47	reclamation	16	rite	11
preconceive	43	pronunciation	43	reconsider	1	ritual	11
preconception	43	propellant	48	reduce	7, 42	rupture	26
predate	2	propose	41	reduction	7	salvageable	47
predetermine	2	proposition	41	referent	48	scoreless	4
predict	5	prospect	24	referred	48	secede	42
predictable	46	protract	26	reflect	27	secession	42
prediction	5	protrude	8	reflex	27	sectarian	37
preexisting	2	protrusion	8	reform	1	senator	19
preference	48	provocation	35	refract	27	senatorial	19
preferred	48	provocative	35	regenerate	34	sensor	37
prefix	2	provoke	35	regress	26	sentient	37
prejudge	2	pseudonym	34	reinstall	1	sentiment	37
prejudice	17, 29	psychiatry	35	reject	27	serene	11
prejudicial	17	psycholinguistics	35	remedial	37	serenity	11
preoccupied	2	psychology	35	remedy	37	serpentine	36
preposition	2, 41	psychopathology	35	remembrance	35	shinier	3
prescribe	28	public	17	remit	27	shiniest	3

sign	9	sufficient	14	telepathy	37	tricolor	20
signature	9	suffix	50	telephone	22	triennial	20
similar	12	suggest	6	telephoto	22	trigonometry	20
similarity	12	suggestion	6	telescope	22	trilogy	20
sinusitis	36	supercomputer	21	television	22	triplets	20
sociolinguist	35	superhero	21	tetrad	23	tripod	20
soft	9	superhighway	21	tetralogy	23	trivial	18
soften	9	superhuman	21	tetrapod	23	triviality	18
solemn	9	superimpose	21	tetrarchy	23	tutor	15
solemnity	9	supportable	24, 50	thermometer	22	tutorial	15
soliloquy	37	suppress	40	thoughtless	4	type	10
solitaire	37	suppression	50	thoughtlessness	4	typical	10
solitary	37	suspend	40	tonsillitis	36	unattached	1
solitude	37	sustain	43	toxic	17	undesirable	47
specific	14	sustainable	46	toxicity	17	unglued	1
specify	14	sustenance	43	traction	26	unheated	1
spectacle	24	syllabic	18	tractor	26	unnamable	47
spectacular	24	sympathy	37	trajectory	27	unopened	1
spectator	24	symphony	22	transcribe	28	unplanned	1
spectrum	24	synonym	34	transfusion	40	unpredictable	25
stable	41	tactful	4	transgress	26	unread	1
statistics	41	tactless	4	translate	7	verdict	25
stranger	3	tactlessness	4	translation	7	version	38
strangest	3	technical	17	transmit	27	vertigo	38
submission	8, 27	technician	17	transpire	38	viaduct	42
submit	8, 27	technocracy	31	transport	24	vocabulary	35
substitute	41	technocrat	31	triangle	20	vocal	35
subtract	5	technophobic	36	triathlon	20	vocalic	35
subtraction	5	telecommunication		tricentennial	20	volcanic	11
succeed	42		22	trickier	3	volcano	11
suffice	14	telegraph	22	trickiest	3	xenophobia	36